THE COMPUTER SCIENCE LIBRARY

Artificial Intelligence Series
NILS. J. NILSSON, *Editor*

Studies in Automatic Programming Logic

Studies in Automatic Programming Logic

Zohar Manna

Richard Waldinger

with contributions by

Shmuel Katz and Karl Levitt

NORTH-HOLLAND·NEW YORK

NEW YORK · AMSTERDAM · OXFORD

Elsevier North-Holland, Inc.
52 Vanderbilt Avenue, New York, New York 10017

North-Holland Publishing Company
P.O. Box 211
Amsterdam, The Netherlands

Library of Congress Cataloging in Publication Data

Manna, Zohar.
   Studies in automatic programming logic.
   (Artificial intelligence series) (The
computer science library)
   Bibliography: p.
   Includes index.
   1. Electronic digital computers—Programming.
2. Computer programs. I. Waldinger, Richard,
joint author. II. Title.
QA76.6.M357   001.6'42   77-5765
ISBN 0-444-00224-3
ISBN 0-444-00225-1 pbk.

Manufactured in the United States of America

Contents

Preface

As computers have developed, they have come to play a larger and larger role in the programming process. Although twenty-five years ago programmers had to express their programs as sequences of numbers, and to interpret similarly encrypted error messages, today they are assisted by a battalion of assemblers, compilers, editors, interactive debuggers, and other tools by which the machine aids in its own programming. The next stage in the progression is likely to be the appearance of systems that can understand the subject matter of the program being constructed, and thus play a more critical and active role in its development. A compiler, for instance, can detect a syntactic error such as a missing *plus* sign, but it cannot hope to recognize a logical error, such as when a *plus* sign has been replaced by a *minus.* To detect such a mistake, a system must understand the program more thoroughly than the compiler does. In recent years, experimental systems with this level of understanding have begun to appear.

The three papers in this collection illustrate how intelligent systems can be applied to the verification, debugging, and synthesis of computer programs:

Reasoning About Programs (by R. Waldinger and K. Levitt) describes a computer system to prove the correctness of a given program.

Logical Analysis of Programs (by S. Katz and Z. Manna) presents techniques for the automatic documentation of given programs to assist in their debugging or verification.

Knowledge and Reasoning in Program Synthesis (by Z. Manna and R. Waldinger) suggests methods for the automatic development of computer programs.

This collection treats, a progression of tasks of increasing complexity. In the first paper, we attempt to show that a given program is consistent with given specifications and documentation, in the form of "invariant assertions." In the second paper, we begin with only the program and its specifications, and we introduce means to generate the documentation of the program and to correct the program if the specifications are not met. In the final paper, we assume that only the specifications are given, and we propose techniques for developing a program guaranteed to meet the specifications.

Progress in the implementation of these techniques reflects the increasing complexity of their corresponding tasks and the ingenuity they require. Program verification has been studied intensely, and our first paper actually describes a running verification system. (The description of the system is exceptionally complete, containing as an appendix a full annotated listing of the theorem prover and traces of sample solutions. Thus, a reader who is interested in actually implementing a verification system can see exactly how it was done.) On the other hand, debugging and synthesis are not yet so well understood, and the methods in our second and third papers have only been partially implemented.

The three papers have appeared earlier in journals, but are presented here in a corrected, updated, and slightly modified form. "Reasoning about programs" appeared in the journal *Artifical Intelligence* (Vol. 5, No. 3, Fall 1974, pp. 235–316), "Logical analysis of Programs" in the *Communications of the ACM* (Vol. 19, No. 4, Apr. 1976, pp. 188–206), and "Knowledge and reasoning in program synthesis" in *Artifical Intelligence* (Vol. 6, No. 2, Summer 1975, pp. 175–208). We are indebted to these journals for permission to reprint the papers in this collection. In the subsequent postscript we summarize more recent developments briefly. The references have been combined into a single bibliography at the end.

Z. M. and R. W.

Chapter 1
Reasoning About Programs

Richard Waldinger and Karl Levitt

> Problems worthy
> of attack
> Prove their worth
> by hitting back.
> *Piet Hein*

1. Introduction and Background

This paper describes a computer system that proves theorems about programs, a task of practical importance because it helps certify that the programs are correct. Instead of testing a program on test cases, which may allow some bugs to remain, we can try to prove mathematically that it behaves as we expect.

Many programs have done this sort of reasoning. King's (1969) program verifier proved an interesting class of theorems and was very fast. Deutsch's (1973) system is perhaps not as fast as King's, but it can prove more interesting theorems. Igarashi et al. (1975) applied a resolution theorem prover to the verification of programs written in PASCAL, such as Hoare's (1961) FIND. Their system does little actual resolution but a lot of simplification and reasoning about equality. A program devised by Boyer and Moore (1975) can prove difficult theorems about LISP programs.

Thus there is no shortage of interesting work related to our own. The special characteristic of our system is that it is markedly

This is a revised version of a previously published article by the same name which appeared in *Artificial Intelligence,* vol 5, pp. 235-316. Copyright 1974 by North-Holland Publishing Company, Amsterdam. Reprinted here by permission of publisher.

concise, readable, and easy to change and apply to new subject areas.

Our program verifier consists of a *theorem prover* (or *deductive system*) and a *verification condition generator*. The verification condition generator takes an annotated program as input and constructs a list of theorems as output. The truth of the constructed theorems implies the correctness of the program. The task of the deductive system is to prove these theorems. The verification condition generator (Elspas et al., 1973) is written in INTERLISP (Teitelman, 1975), and the deductive system is written in QA4 (Rulifson et al, 1972). This paper focuses on the deductive system but, to be complete, gives examples of verification condition generation as well.

In writing our deductive system, we were motivated by several goals. First, the system should be able to find proofs; it should have enough deductive power to prove, within a comfortable time and space, the theorems being considered. Also, these proofs should be at the level of an informal demonstration in a mathematical textbook. This means that the difficulty in following one line to the next in any proof should be small enough that the proof is understandable, yet large enough not to be trivial. In any practical program verifier, the user will wish to follow the steps in a deduction. Furthermore, the strategies the system uses in searching for a proof should be strategies that we find natural. Not only should the tactics that eventually lead to the proof be ones we might use in proving the statement by hand, but also the false starts the system makes should be ones we might make ourselves. We do not want the system to rely on blind search; the trace of an attempted solution should make interesting reading.

In addition to the requirement that proofs be readable, the rules the system uses in going from one line to the next should be easy to read and understand. We should be able to look at a rule and see what it does. Also, it should be easy to change old rules and to add new rules. The user of a program verifier is likely to introduce new concepts, such as operators or data structures. We want to be able to tell the deductive system how these structures behave and to have the system reason effectively using the new symbols. Giving the system new information should be possible without knowing how the system works, and certainly without reprogramming it. Furthermore, the addition of new information should not degrade the performance of the system prohibitively.

The system is intended to evolve with use. As we apply the system to new problems, we are forced to give it new information and, perhaps, to generalize some old information. These changes are incorporated into the system, which may then be better able to solve new problems.

Since the system is easy to extend and generalize, we do not worry about the completeness or generality of any particular version of the system. It is powerful enough to solve the sort of problem on which it has been trained, and it can be easily changed when necessary.

These considerations played a part in the design of the programming system called QA4, as well as the construction of our deductive system, which is written in the QA4 language. Some of the techniques described below are embedded in the QA4 system itself; others are expressed as parts of the deductive system.

2. The Method

Perhaps not all readers are familiar with the method of proving statements about programs that we have followed in our work. Our method is a natural technique introduced independently by Floyd (1967) and Naur (1966) and formalized by Hoare (1969). Knuth (1968, pp 17–18) traces the germ of the idea back to von Neumann and Goldstine (1963). An other presentation of the same idea appears in a lecture by Turing (1950). Although we cannot give a thorough introduction to the technique here, we provide below an example of its application to convey the flavor of the approach.

2.1. A Straight-Line Program

Consider a simple program, written in a flowchart language, that exchanges the values of two variables, as shown in Figure 1.1. We assume that before the program is executed, X and Y have some initial values X_0 and Y_0. Suppose we want to prove that after the program is executed, $X = Y_0$ and $Y = X_0$. Then we offer the *input* and *output assertions* as comments in our program shown in Figure

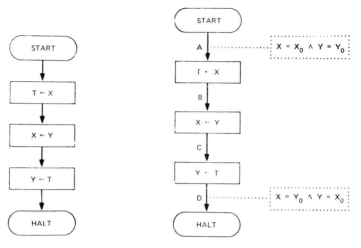

Figure 1.1.   Figure 1.2.

1.2. These assertions are not to be executed by the program, but they tell us something about the way the programmer expects his program to behave. He expects the assertion at A to be true when control passes through A, and the assertion at D to be true when control passes through D.

The essence of the approach is to generate from a commented program like the one above a set of statements called the *verification conditions*. If these statements and the input assertion are true, then the other assertions the programmer has put in his program are correct. Whereas the programmer's assertions are intended to hold only when control passes through the appropriate point, the verification conditions should be true in general, and they can be proved by a deductive system that knows nothing about sequential processing, loops, recursion, or other concepts about the flow of control of the particular program.

To generate the verification condition for our sample program, we pass the output assertion back toward the input assertion. As we pass it back, we change it to reflect the changing state of the system. In particular, if any assignments are made within the program, then the corresponding substitution should be made in the assertion. Passing the assignment at D back to point C changes it to $X = Y_0$ and $T = X_0$, as shown in Figure 1.3. We can argue that if the assertion at C

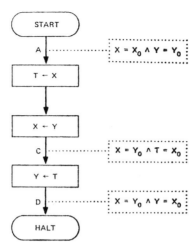

Figure 1.3.

is true when control passes through C, then the assertion at D will be true when control passes through D. In particular, if $T = X_0$ is true at C, and we execute $Y \leftarrow T$, then $Y = X_0$ will be true at D.

Passing the assertion all the way back to A in this manner gives the assertion $Y = Y_0 \wedge X = X_0$. If this assertion is true at A, then the final assertion will be true at D. However, we are already given the initial assertion $X = X_0 \wedge Y = Y_0$. The truth of the assertion at D then depends on the truth of the obvious implication $X = X_0 \wedge Y = Y_0 \supset Y = Y_0 \wedge X = X_0$. This statement is the verification condition for this program. It can be proved by a deductive system independently of any knowledge about this program.

Constructing verification conditions by this method is an algorithmic process, not a heuristic one. On the other hand, there can be no cut and dried algorithm for proving such verification conditions. However, the somewhat restricted domain of program verification is more tractable than the general theorem-proving problem.

2.2. A Loop Program

Before we explain how the system is structured or implemented, let us first look at some examples of how verification conditions are generated and proved by our system. This example will give a better

idea of the subject domain of the inference system and of the sort
of reasoning it has to do.

Suppose we are given the annotated program shown in Figure 1.4
to compute the largest element in an array and its location. This
program searches through the array, keeping track of the largest
element it has seen so far and the location of this element. The
intermediate assertion[1] at C says that MAX is the largest element
in the array between 0 and I and that LOC is the index for MAX.
Although our assertion language does not permit the ellipsis notation
("..."), we have introduced some suitable analogues, which are
discussed later.

To prove assertions about a complex program, the system decom-
poses it into simple paths. This program can be decomposed into
four simple paths:

(1) The path from B to C.
(2) The path from C to D.
(3) The path from C around the loop and back to C through
    point E.
(4) The path from C around the loop and back to C through
    point F.

Notice that the author of this program has put assertions not only
at the START and HALT nodes of the program, but also at the
intermediate point C. He has done this so that the proof of the program can be reduced to proving straight-line paths in the same way
that the simple program of the previous section was verified. For
instance, the path that begins at C, travels around the loop through
E, and returns to C can be regarded as a simple, straight-line program
with the assertion at C as both its start assertion and its halt assertion. The assertion at C has been cleverly chosen to be true when the
loop is entered and to remain true whenever control travels around
the loop and returns to C, and to allow the assertion at D to be
proved when control leaves the loop and the program halts. The
choice of suitable internal assertions can be an intellectually exacting

---

[1] In this program, and in examples throughout the paper, when we list several statements
in an assertion, we mean the implicit conjunction of those statements. We will often also
refer to each conjunct as an "assertion".

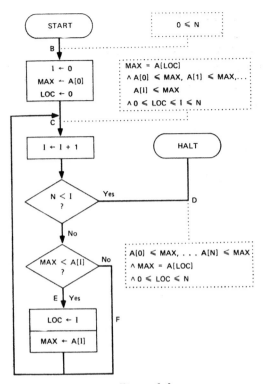

Figure 1.4.

task; some heuristic methods have been proposed that will work in this and many other examples (Elspas, 1974; Wegbreit, 1974; German and Wegbreit, 1975; Katz and Manna, 1976).

If all the straight-line paths of the program are shown to be correctly described by the given assertions, and if the program can be shown to terminate (this must be done separately), then we can conclude that the program is indeed correct, at least with respect to the programmer's final assertion.

Although there are many paths in the decomposition of a program, typically most of the paths are easy to verify. For this program, we examine two of the paths.

2.2.1. Verifying One Path

First, suppose we want to demonstrate that if the assertion at point C is true when control passes through C, then the assertion at

C will still be true if control passes around the loop and returns again to C. We will restrict our attention to the more interesting case, in which the test MAX $<$ A[I]? is true; in this case, control passes through E. Furthermore, we will try to prove only that the second conjunct of the assertion at C remains true. Our verification condition generator gives us the following statement to prove:

$$MAX = A[LOC] \quad \wedge \tag{1.1}$$

$$A[0] \leqslant MAX, ..., A[I] \leqslant MAX \quad \wedge \tag{1.2}$$

$$0 \leqslant LOC \leqslant I \leqslant N \quad \wedge \tag{1.3}$$

$$\neg (N < I + 1) \quad \wedge \tag{1.4}$$

$$MAX < A[I + 1] \quad \supset \tag{1.5}$$

$$A[0] \leqslant A[I + 1], ..., A[I + 1] \leqslant A[I + 1]. \tag{1.6}$$

This statement is actually represented as five separate hypotheses and a goal to be deduced from these hypotheses. Lines (1.1) through (1.3) come from the assertion at C, and lines (1.4) and (1.5) come from the tests along the path. Line (1.6) comes from the assertion at C again. How the above statement is derived from the program is shown in detail below.

The behavior of the deductive system in this problem is typical of its approach to many problems. The goal (1.6) is broken into two subgoals:

$$A[0] \leqslant A[I + 1] \quad \wedge \quad \cdots \quad \wedge \quad A[I] \leqslant A[I + 1] \tag{1.7}$$

and

$$A[I + 1] \leqslant A[I + 1]. \tag{1.8}$$

The second subgoal, (1.8), is immediately seen to be true. The first subgoal, (1.7), is easily derived from (1.2) and (1.5).

2.2.2. Generating a Verification Condition

For those readers unfamiliar with the Floyd method of producing verification conditions, we give an example of its application: a complete trace of how the above verification condition was produced.

The path under consideration begins at point C, travels around the loop through point E, and returns again to C. We will try to prove the second conjunct at C.

This statement is

$$A[0] \leqslant MAX, \quad A[1] \leqslant MAX, \quad ..., \quad A[I] \leqslant MAX. \quad (1.9)$$

We pass this assertion backward around the loop to point E, making the corresponding substitution. The transformed assertion is then

$$A[0] \leqslant A[I], \quad A[1] \leqslant A[I], \quad ..., \quad A[I] \leqslant A[I]. \quad (1.10)$$

Since LOC does not appear explicitly in (1.10), the assignment LOC ← I has no effect.

To reach point E, the test

$$MAX < A[I]? \quad (1.11)$$

must have been true. Passing the assertion back before the test gives the implication

$$MAX < A[I] \quad \supset \quad A[0] \leqslant A[I], A[1] \leqslant A[I], ..., A[I] \leqslant A[I].$$

$$(1.12)$$

If this implication is true before the test (1.11), the assertion (1.10) will be true after the test. To travel around the loop at all, the result of the test

$$N < I? \quad (1.13)$$

must have been false. Passing the assertion (1.12) back over the test (1.13) gives

$$\neg (N < I) \wedge MAX < A[I]$$

$$\supset \quad A[0] \leqslant A[I], A[1] \leqslant A[I], ..., A[I] \leqslant A[I]. \quad (1.14)$$

Passing (1.14) back over the assignment statement

$$I \leftarrow I + 1 \quad (1.15)$$

gives

$$\neg (N < I + 1) \wedge MAX < A[I + 1]$$

$$\supset \quad A[0] \leqslant A[I + 1], A[1] \leqslant A[I + 1], ..., A[I + 1] \leqslant A[I + 1].$$

$$(1.16)$$

This statement has been generated in such a way that if it is true when control passes through point C, then (1.9) will be true if control passes around the loop through point E and returns to C. If we consider this path as a straight-line program with the assertion at C as both its start assertion and its halt assertion, then proving the correctness of the second conjunct (1.9) at C reduces to proving

$$\text{MAX} = A[\text{LOC}] \quad \wedge$$

$$A[0] \leqslant \text{MAX}, ..., A[I] \leqslant \text{MAX} \quad \wedge$$

$$0 \leqslant \text{LOC} \leqslant I \leqslant N \quad \wedge$$

$$\neg (N < I + 1) \quad \wedge$$

$$\text{MAX} < A[I + 1] \qquad \supset$$

$$A[0] \leqslant A[I + 1], ..., A[I + 1] \leqslant A[I + 1].$$

Finally, the antecedents of this implication are expressed as separate hypotheses, and the consequent is represented as a goal. This is exactly the condition that was proved in the previous section.

2.2.3. Verifying Another Path

Now let us look more briefly at the path from C to D. We will assume the assertion at C is true and will prove the assertion at D. We will look at the first conjunct of the assertion at D. Our verification condition generator gives us the following statement to prove:

$$\text{MAX} = A[\text{LOC}] \quad \wedge \tag{1.17}$$

$$A[0] \leqslant \text{MAX} \wedge \cdots \wedge A[I] \leqslant \text{MAX} \quad \wedge \tag{1.18}$$

$$0 \leqslant \text{LOC} \leqslant I \leqslant N \quad \wedge \tag{1.19}$$

$$N < I + 1 \qquad \supset \tag{1.20}$$

$$A[0] \leqslant \text{MAX} \wedge \cdots \wedge A[N] \leqslant \text{MAX}. \tag{1.21}$$

The reasoning required for this proof is a little more subtle than the previous deduction. When the system learns that $N < I+1$ (1.20), it immediately concludes that $N + 1 \leqslant I + 1$, since N and I are integers. It further deduces that $N \leqslant I$. Since it already knows that $I \leqslant N$ (1.19), it concludes that $N = I$. Using the hypothesis (1.18), the system reduces the goal (1.21) to proving that $I = N$, which it now knows.

This deduction involves a lot of reasoning forward from assumptions, while the preceding deduction required reasoning backward from goals. Both of these proofs are typical of the behavior of the system at large in their use of the properties of equality and the ordering relations.

In reading the QA4 listing of the theorem prover (Section 6), one is struck by the absence of any general deductive mechanisms outside of the language processor itself. The QA4 system incorporates enough of the common techniques of theorem proving and problem solving that our inference system needs no general problem-solving knowledge, but only some knowledge about numbers, arrays, and other structures. The following sections show how the QA4 language allows that knowledge to be represented.

3. The Language

3.1. Pattern Matching and the Goal Mechanism

The deductive system is made up of many rules expressed as small functions or programs. Each of these programs knows one fact and the use for that fact. The QA4 programming language is designed so that all these programs can be coordinated; when a problem is presented to the system, the functions that are relevant to the problem "stand forward" in the sense explained below.

A program has the form

$$(\text{LAMBDA} \ \langle\text{pattern}\rangle \ \langle\text{body}\rangle).$$

Part of the knowledge of what the program can be used for is expressed in the pattern. When a function is applied to an argument, the pattern is matched against that argument. If the argument turns out to be an instance of the pattern, the match is said to be successful. The unbound variables in the pattern are then bound to the appropriate subexpressions of the argument, and the body of the program is evaluated with respect to those new bindings.

For example, the program

$$\text{REVTUP} = (\text{LAMBDA} \ (\text{TUPLE} \leftarrow X \leftarrow Y) \ (\text{TUPLE} \ \$Y \ \$X))$$

has pattern (TUPLE $\leftarrow X \leftarrow Y$) and body (TUPLE \$Y \$X). The symbol "TUPLE" is treated as a constant, and can only be matched against itself. The prefix "$\leftarrow$" means that the variable is to be given a new binding. The prefix "$" means that the variable's old binding is to be used. When REVTUP is applied to (TUPLE A B), the pattern (TUPLE ←X ←Y) is matched against (TUPLE A B). The match is seen to be successful, the variable X is bound to A and the variable Y is bound to B. The body (TUPLE $Y $X) is evaluated with respect to these bindings, giving (TUPLE B A).

On the other hand, if a function is applied to an argument and the pattern of that function does not match the argument, a condition known as *failure* occurs. At many points in the execution of a program, the system makes an arbitrary choice between alternatives. Failure initiates a backing up to the most recent choice and the selection of another alternative, if one exists. The mismatching of patterns is only one of the ways in which failure can occur in a program.

We have yet to explain how a program stands forward when it is relevant. In the above example, the function was called by name, much as it is in a conventional programming language. But it is also possible to make an argument available to any applicable program in a specified class. This is done by means of the *goal mechanism*.

When we say (GOAL ⟨goalclass⟩ ⟨argument⟩), where the goal class is a tuple of names of functions, we first check to see whether the argument is known to be true, in which case the statement succeeds. Otherwise that argument becomes available to the entire goal class. The pattern of each of those functions is matched in turn against the argument. If the match is successful, the function is applied to that argument. If the function returns a value, that value is returned as the value of the goal statement. On the other hand, if the match of the pattern fails, or if a failure occurs in evaluating the function, backtracking takes place, the next function in the goal class is tried, and the process is repeated. If none of the functions in the goal class succeed, the entire goal statement fails.

For example, in our deductive system, one of the goal classes is called EQRULES, the rules used for proving equalities. One of these rules is

EQTIMESDIVIDE =
    (LAMBDA (EQ ←W (TIMES (DIVIDE ←X ←Y) ←Z))
       (GOAL $EQRULES
          (EQ (TIMES $Y $W)(TIMES $X $Z)))).

This rule states that to prove W = (X/Y)*Z, we should try to prove Y*W = X*Z. It is assumed (for simplicity) that Y will not be 0. (The actual EQTIMESDIVIDE, shown in Section 6, is more general than this.) The rule has the pattern

(EQ ←W (TIMES (DIVIDE ←X ←Y) ←Z)).

If we execute (GOAL $EQRULES (EQ A (TIMES (DIVIDE B C) D))) [i.e., we want to prove A = (B/C)*D], the system will try all the applicable EQRULES in turn. If none of the previous rules succeed, the system will eventually reach EQTIMESDIVIDE. It will find that the pattern of EQTIMESDIVIDE matches this argument, binding W to A, X to B, Y to C, and Z to D. Then it will evaluate the body of this function; i.e., it will try

(GOAL $EQRULES (EQ (TIMES A C) (TIMES B D))).

If it succeeds at proving (EQ (TIMES A C) (TIMES B D)), it will return normally. If it fails, it will try to apply the remaining EQRULES to the original argument, (EQ A (TIMES (DIVIDE B C) D)). The goal statement is an example of the pattern-directed function invocation introduced by Hewitt (1971) in PLANNER.

The net effect of this mechanism is that it enables the user to write his programs in terms of what he wants done, without needing to specify how he wants to do it. Furthermore, at any point, he can add new rules to EQRULES or any other goal class, thus increasing the power of the system with little effort.

3.2. Some Sample Rules

The deductive system is a collection of rules represented as small programs. One rule was given in the preceding section; two more rules are presented here. The complete deductive system is included in Section 6.

The first rule, EQSIMP, attempts to prove an equality by simplifying its arguments:

```
EQSIMP = (LAMBDA (EQ ←X ←Y)
            (PROG (DECLARE)
                  (SETQ ←X ($SIMPONE $X))
                  (GOAL $EQRULES (EQ $X $Y)))
            BACKTRACK).
```

This rule says: to prove an equality, try to simplify one side of
the equality. The rule, a member of EQRULES, has the pattern
(EQ ←X ←Y). It is applicable to a goal of form (EQ A B), where A
and B are any expressions. When EQSIMP is applied to such a goal, X
will bound to A and Y to B. SIMPONE, the simplifier, will simplify
A. The goal statement tries to prove that the simplified A is equal to
B. If it succeeds, the rule will return in the ordinary way. If the goal
statement fails, or if the simplifier fails to simplify A, the entire
application of the rule will fail.

The predicate EQ implicitly takes a set as its argument (see Section 3.4). Thus, there is an alternative match of (EQ ←X ←Y) to
(EQ A B), binding X to B and Y to A. The user has specified the
BACKTRACK option, meaning that he wants to try all possible
matches. Therefore, if the first application of EQSIMP fails, the
system will apply it the other way and try to simplify B. Only if
this second attempt fails will the entire rule fail, allowing other
members of EQRULES to work on the same goal.

The second rule is

FSUBTRACTI = (LAMBDA (←F (SUBTRACT ←X ←Y) ←Z)
                       (GOAL $INEQUALITIES
                        ($F $X (PLUS $Y $Z))))).

This rule says: to prove $X-Y \leq Z$, try to prove $X \leq Y + Z$. It belongs
to the goal class INEQUALITIES and is thus used not only for the
predicate LTQ ($\leq$), but also for LT ($<$), GT ($>$), and GTQ ($\geq$). The
variable F is bound to the appropriate predicate symbol when
the pattern is matched against the goal.

3.3. Demons

The goal mechanism is used for reasoning backward from a goal.
However, sometimes we want to reason forward from a statement.
For example, suppose that whenever an assertion of the form $X \geq Y$
is asserted, we want to assert $Y \leq X$ as well. We do this by a QA4
mechanism known as the *demon*.

A demon is imagined to be a spirit that inhabits a hiding place,
waiting until some specified event occurs, at which time it appears,
performs some action, and vanishes again. We have put several
demons in the system, each watching for a different condition. For

instance, one demon watches for statements of the form $X \geqslant Y$ and makes the statement $Y \leqslant X$. The user of the system can create his own demons. Demons are a tool for reasoning forward from an antecedent. In particular, we use demons to drive antecedents into a canonical form. For example, we drive all inequality expressions with integer arguments into an assertion of the form $X \leqslant Y$.

3.4. Representations

To as great an extent as possible, we have chosen representations that model the semantics of the concepts we use so as to make our deductions shorter and easier. For example, our language has data structures especially intended to eliminate the need for certain inferences. In addition to *tuples*, which are like the familiar lists of the list-processing languages, we have the finite *sets* of conventional mathematics, and *bags*, which are unordered tuples or, equivalently, sets that may have multiple occurrences of the same element. [Bags are called multisets by Knuth (1969), who outlines many of their properties.] Furthermore, we allow arbitrary expressions to have property lists in the same way that atoms can have property lists in LISP (McCarthy et al., 1962).

These data structures are useful in the modeling of equivalence relations, ordering relations, and arithmetic functions. For instance, if the addition of numbers and the multiplication of numbers are each represented by a function of two arguments, then it becomes necessary to use numerous applications of the commutative and associative laws to prove anything about the number system. However, in QA4 all functions take only one argument, but this argument can be a tuple, set, or bag, as well as any other expression. Functions of multiple arguments can be represented by a function defined on tuples. However, a function that is commutative and associative, such as PLUS, is defined on bags. The expression (PLUS A 2 B) really means (PLUS (BAG A 2 B)). Recall that bags are unordered; the system cannot distinguish between (BAG A 2 B) and (BAG 2 A B). Consequently, the expressions (PLUS A 2 B) and (PLUS 2 A B) are identically equal in our system. This makes the commutative law for addition redundant and, in fact, inexpressible in the language. Most needs for the associative law are also avoided.

The logical function AND has the property that, for instance, (AND A A B) = (AND A B). The number of occurrences of an argument does not affect its value. Consequently, AND takes a set as its argument. Since (SET A A B) and (SET A B) are indistinguishable, (AND A A B) and (AND A B) are identical, and a statement of their equality is unneccessary. Some functions that take sets as arguments are AND, OR, EQ, and GCD (greatest common divisor).

When a new fact is asserted to our system, the value TRUE is placed on the property list of that fact. If at some later time we want to know if that fact is true, we simply look on its property list.

However, certain facts are given special handling in addition. For example, if we tell the system that certain expressions are equal, we form a set of those expressions. On the property list of each expression, we place a pointer to that set. For instance, if we assert (EQ A B C), the system stores the following:

If we subsequently discover any of these expressions to be equal to still another expression, the system adds the new expression to the previously formed set and puts the set on the property list of the new expression as well. For instance, if we assert (EQ B D), our structure is changed to the following:

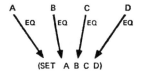

The transitivity, symmetry, and reflexivity of equality are thus implicit in our representation. If we ask whether A and D are equal, the system knows immediately by looking at the property list of A or D.

Ordering relations are also stored using the property-list mechanism. If we know that some expression A is less than B, we place a pointer to B on the property list of A:

$$A \xrightarrow{\text{LT}} B.$$

If we learn that B is less than C, we put a pointer to C on the property list of B:

$$A \xrightarrow{\text{LT}} B \xrightarrow{\text{LT}} C.$$

If we then ask the system if A is less than C, it will search along the pointers in the appropriate way to answer affirmatively. The transitive law is built into this representation.

The system knows about LT ($<$), GT ($>$), LTQ ($\leqslant$), GTQ ($\geqslant$), EQ ($=$), NEQ ($\neq$), and how these relations interact. For example, if we assert $X \geqslant Y$, $Y \geqslant Z$, and $X \leqslant Z$, the system will know $X = Y = Z$ and that $(F\ X\ A) = (F\ Y\ A)$ for any function symbol F and argument A. Or if we assert $X \geqslant Y$ and $X \neq Y$, the system will know $X > Y$.

3.5. Contexts

When we are trying to prove an implication of the form $A \supset B$, it is natural to want to prove B under the hypothesis that A is true. Our assumption of the truth of A holds only as long as we are trying to prove B; after the proof of B is complete, we want to forget that we have assumed A. For this and other reasons, the QA4 language contains a context mechanism. All assertions are made with respect to a context, either implicitly or explicitly. For any context, we can create an arbitrary number of lower contexts.

A query made with respect to a context will have access to all assertions made with respect to higher contexts but not to any assertions made with respect to any other contexts. For instance, suppose we are trying to prove $i < j \supset i + 1 \leqslant j$ with respect to some context C_0. We may have already made some assertions in context C_0. We establish a lower context, C_1, and assert $i < j$ with respect to C_1. Then we try to prove $i + 1 \leqslant j$ with respect to C_1. When proving $i + 1 \leqslant j$, we know $i < j$, as well as all the assertions we knew previously in C_0. When the proof of $i + 1 \leqslant j$ is complete, we may have other statements to prove in C_0. In doing these proofs, we will know all the assertions in C_0 and also, perhaps, the assertion $i < j \supset i + 1 \leqslant j$, but we will not know $i < j$ because it was asserted with respect to a lower context.

3.6. User Interaction

Sometimes our rules ask whether they should continue or fail. This allows a user to cut off lines of reasoning that he knows in advance are fruitless. If he makes a mistake in aswering the question, he may cause the system to fail when it could have succeeded. However, he can never cause the system to find a false or erroneous proof.

In addition to these mechanisms, which are built into the language processor, we have developed some notations that make it easier to describe programming constructs; these notations are a part of our assertion language and are interpreted by the deductive system.

3.7. Notation

In speaking about the program to find the maximum element of an array, we found it convenient to use the ellipsis notation ("..."). We have not introduced this notation into our assertion language; however, we have found ways of getting around its absence.

3.7.1. TUPA, SETA, BAGA

Let A be a one-dimensional array and I and J be integers. Then (TUPA A I J) is the tuple

$$(\text{TUPLE } A[I], A[I + 1], ..., A[J]).$$

If $I > J$, then (TUPA A I J) is the empty tuple.

(SETA A I J) and (BAGA A I J) are the corresponding bag and set. To state that an array is sorted between 0 and N, we assert

$$(\text{LTQ (TUPA A 0 N))}.$$

To state that an array A is the same in contents between 0 and N as the initial array A_0, although these contents may have been permuted, we assert

$$(\text{EQ (BAGA A 0 N) (BAGA } A_0 \text{ 0 N))}.$$

3.7.2. The STRIP Operator

Let X be a set or bag, $X = (SET\ X_1, ..., X_n)$, or $X = (BAG\ X_1, ..., X_n)$. Then (LTQ (STRIP X) Y) means $X_1 \leqslant Y$ and ... and $X_n \leqslant Y$. For instance, to state that MAX is greater than or equal to any element in an array A between I and J, we assert

$$(LTQ\ (STRIP\ (BAGA\ A\ I\ J))\ MAX).$$

This is perhaps not quite so clear as

$$A[I] \leqslant MAX,\quad A[I+1] \leqslant MAX,\quad ...,\quad A[J] \leqslant MAX,$$

but we prefer it to the first-order predicate calculus notation,

$$(\forall u)[(I \leqslant u \wedge u \leqslant J) \quad \supset \quad A[u] \leqslant MAX].$$

The STRIP operator is also used to remove parentheses from expressions:

$$(BAG\ A\ (STRIP\ (BAG\ B\ C\ D)))$$

is

$$(BAG\ A\ B\ C\ D).$$

We will eventually need two distinct operators, one to act as a quantifier and one to remove parentheses, but the single operator STRIP has played both roles so far.

3.7.3. Access and Change

Arrays cannot be treated as functions, because their contents can be changed, whereas functions do not change their definitions. Thus, while f(x) is likely to mean the same thing for the same value of x at different times, A[x] is not. We overcome this difficulty by adopting McCarthy (1962) functions[2] ACCESS and CHANGE in our

---

[2] They are actually called c and a ("contents" and "assign") in that paper. We follow King (1969), who inadvertently reversed the roles of the initials.

explication of the array concept:

> (ACCESS A I) means A[I].
> (CHANGE A I T) means the array A after the assignment
>   statement A[I]←T has been executed.

We do not propose that ACCESS and CHANGE be used in writing programs or assertions; we do find that they make reasoning about arrays simpler, as King suspected they would.

The next section shows examples of some fairly difficult proofs produced by the deductive system. The actual traces for some of these are included in Section 7.

4. Examples

4.1. The Real-Number Quotient Algorithm

Very little work has been done to prove properties of programs that work on the real numbers or the floating-point numbers, although there is no reason to believe such proofs could not be done. Figure 1.5 shows, for instance, a program (Wensley, 1958) to compute an approximate quotient Y of real numbers P and Q, where $0 \leqslant P < Q$. This is an interesting computationally plausible algorithm. It uses only addition, subtraction, and division by 2, and it computes a new significant bit of the quotient with each iteration.

The algorithm can be understood in the following way. At the beginning of each iteration, P/Q belongs to the half-open interval [Y, Y + D). It is determined whether P/Q belongs to the left half or the right half of the interval. if P/Q is in the right half, Y is reset to Y + D/2; otherwise, Y is let alone. Then D is halved. Thus P/Q remains in the interval [Y, Y + D), and Y becomes a better and better approximation for P/Q. Initially, Y is 0 and D is 1. The variables A and B retain certain intermediate values to make the computation more efficient.

We will consider here only one path through this program, i.e., the path around the loop that follows the right branch of the test $P < A + B$. We will prove only one loop assertion: $P < Y*Q + D*Q$. Our verification condition generator supplies us with the following

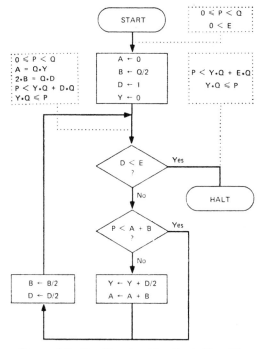

Figure 1.5. The Wensley Quotient Algorithm.

hypotheses:

$$0 \leqslant P, \tag{1.22}$$

$$P < Q, \tag{1.23}$$

$$A = Q*Y, \tag{1.24}$$

$$2*B = Q*D, \tag{1.25}$$

$$P < Y*Q + D*Q, \tag{1.26}$$

$$Y*Q \leqslant P, \tag{1.27}$$

$$\neg (D < E), \tag{1.28}$$

$$P < A + B. \tag{1.29}$$

The goal is to prove from these hypotheses that

$$P < Q*Y + Q*(D/2). \tag{1.30}$$

These hypotheses and the goal were constructed in a manner precisely analogous to the generation of the condition for the previous example of computing the maximum of an array.

The proof goes as follows. After an abortive attempt at using the assertion (1.26), the system tries to show that the conclusion follows from (1.29). It therefore tries to show that

$$A + B \leqslant Q*Y + Q*(D/2). \tag{1.31}$$

This goal is broken into the following two:

$$A \leqslant Q*Y, \tag{1.32}$$

$$B \leqslant Q*(D/2). \tag{1.33}$$

Of course, this strategy will not always be successful. However, in this case the goal (1.32) follows from (1.24), whereas (1.33) follows from (1.25).

A complete trace of this proof and listings of the rules required to achieve it are provided in the Appendices (Sections 6 and 7).

4.2. A Pattern Matcher

As an experiment in the incorporation of new knowledge into the system, we performed the partial verification of two new examples, a simple pattern matcher and a recursive version of the unification algorithm (Robinson, 1965). These algorithms were of special interest to us because they involve concepts similar to those actually used in the implementation of the QA4 system itself. They are thus in some sense realistic, although neither of these programs appears literally in the QA4 code.

Before we began proving properties of the pattern matcher we had only verified numeric algorithms. With the pattern matcher the system had to be acquainted with a new domain; it had to learn about expressions, substitutions, variables and constants. Therefore this phase of experiment tested the ability of the system to work with a new set of concepts. We will now describe this new domain.

We assume that *expressions* are LISP S-expressions (McCarthy et al., 1962); for example, (F X (G A B)) is an expression. Atomic elements are designated as either *constant* or *variable,* and they can be distinguished by the use of the predicates *const* and *var.* Here we use A, B, C, F, and G as constants and U, V, W, X, Y, and Z as variables:

var(X) is true,
const(A) is true,
var(A) is false,
var((X Y)) is false.

The predicate *constexp* is true if its argument contains no variables:

constexp((A B (X) C)) is false,
constexp((A B (D) C)) is true,
constexp(A) is true.

Note that *constexp,* as distinguished from *const,* can be true even if its argument is nonatomic.

A *substitution* replaces some of the variables of an expression by terms. Substitutions are represented as lists of dotted pairs. ((X · A) (Y · (F G))) is a substitution. *varsubst*(s, e) is the result of making substitution *s* in expression *e*. If *s* is

$$((X · A) (Y · (G B)))),$$

and *e* is

$$(F X A (Y B)),$$

then *varsubst*(s, e) is

$$(F A A ((G B) B)).$$

The LISP functions *car, cdr, list,* and *atom* can be used to manipulate expressions. The empty substitution is denoted by EMPTY and has no effect on an expression. An operation called *compose,* the composition of substitutions, defined by Robinson (1965), has the following property:

varsubst(*compose*(s1, s2), e) = *varsubst*(s1, *varsubst*(s2, e)).

The problem of pattern matching is defined as follows: Given two expressions called the pattern and the argument, try to find a substitution for the variables of the pattern that makes it identical to the argument. We call such a substitution a *match.* For example, if the pattern *pat* is

$$(X (Y A B) X),$$

and the argument *arg* is

$$(D (C A B) D),$$

then *match(pat, arg)* is

$$((X \cdot D) (Y \cdot C)).$$

If there is no substitution that makes the pattern identical to the argument, we want the pattern-matcher to return the distinguished atom NOMATCH. Thus, if *pat* is (X Y X) and *arg* is (A B C), then *match(pat, arg)* = NOMATCH, since we cannot expect X to be matched against both A and C.

For simplicity, we assume that the argument contains no variables. A LISP-like program to perform the match might be

```
match(pat, arg) = prog((m1 m2)
    if const(pat) then (if pat = arg then return(EMPTY)
                                      else return(NOMATCH))
    if var(pat) then return(list(cons(pat, arg)))
    if atom(arg) then return(NOMATCH)
    m1←match(car(pat), car(arg))
    if m1 = NOMATCH then return(NOMATCH)
    m2←match(varsubst(m1, cdr(pat)), cdr(arg))
    if m2 = NOMATCH then return(NOMATCH)
    return(compose(m2, m1)))).
```

The program does the appropriate thing in the case of atomic patterns or arguments, and it calls itself recursively on the left and right halves of the expressions in the nonatomic case. The program applies the substitution found in matching the left halves of the expressions to the right half of the pattern before it is matched, so as to avoid having the same variable matched against different terms.

We have proved several facts about a version of this program, but we focus our attention here on one of them: If the program does not return NOMATCH, then the substitution it finds actually is a match; i.e. applying the substitution to the pattern makes that pattern identical to the argument. Thus, the output assertion is:

$$match(pat, arg) \neq \text{NOMATCH} \supset$$
$$varsubst(match(pat, arg), pat) = arg.$$

Since we assume the argument contains no variables, the input assertion is

$$constexp(arg). \tag{1.34}$$

We have verified one condition for the longest path of *match* with respect to these assertions. This path is followed when the pattern and the argument are both nonatomic and when the recursive calls on *match* successfully return a substitution. In writing our verification condition, we use the same abbreviations the program does, i.e.,

$$m1 = match(car(pat), car(arg)) \tag{1.35}$$

and

$$m2 = match(varsubst(m1, cdr(pat)), cdr(arg)).$$

In proving a property of a recursively defined program, we follow Manna and Pnueli (1970) and assume that property about the recursive call to the program. Thus, for this program we have the inductive hypotheses

$$constexp(car(arg)) \wedge m1 \neq \text{NOMATCH} \supset$$
$$varsubst(m1, car(pat)) = car(arg)$$

(the program works for the *car* of the pattern) and

$$constexp(cdr(arg)) \wedge m2 \neq \text{NOMATCH} \supset$$
$$varsubst(m2, varsubst(m1, cdr(pat))) = cdr(arg) \tag{1.36}$$

(the program works for the instantiated *cdr* of the pattern).[3] The verification condition generator would split both of these hypotheses into three cases; we will consider only the case in which the antecedents of both implications are true. Hence, we assume that both the recursive calls to the pattern matcher succeed in finding matches.

---

[3] Actually, in order to assume the inductive hypotheses we must ensure that the input assertion is satisfied for the recursive calls, in other words, that $constexp(car(arg))$ and $constexp(cdr(arg))$. This follows immediately from the input assertion for the entire program, $constexp(arg)$.

By the path we have taken through the program, we know that

$$\neg const(pat) \tag{1.37}$$

(the pattern is not a constant),

$$\neg var(pat) \tag{1.38}$$

(the pattern is not a variable), and

$$\neg atom(arg) \tag{1.39}$$

(the argument is not an atom). Since for this path

$$match(pat, arg) = compose(m2, m1),$$

the goal is to prove

$$varsubst(compose(m2, m1), pat) = arg. \tag{1.40}$$

The proof produced by the system proceeds as follows. The goal is split into two subgoals:

$$varsubst(compose(m2, m1), car(pat)) = car(arg) \tag{1.41}$$

and

$$varsubst(compose(m2, m1), cdr(pat)) = cdr(arg). \tag{1.42}$$

From the property of *compose,* the first goal is simplified to

$$varsubst(m2, varsubst(m1, car(pat))) = car(arg).$$

Since

$$varsubst(m1, car(pat)) = car(arg)$$

by the first induction hypothesis (1.36), this simplifies to

$$varsubst(m2, car(arg)) = car(arg).$$

Since *arg* contains no variables, neither does *car(arg).* Thus, the goal simplifies to

$$car(arg) = car(arg).$$

The proof of (1.42) is even simpler:

$$varsubst(compose(m2, m1), cdr(pat))$$

simplifies to

$$varsubst(m2, varsubst(m1, cdr(pat))).$$

We know by our second induction hypothesis (1.36) that

$$varsubst(m2, varsubst(m1, cdr(pat))) = cdr(arg),$$

and this completes the proof.

This proof required not only that we add new rules describing the concepts involved, but also that we extend certain of our older capabilities, particularly our ability to simplify expressions using known equalities. A trace of the system's search for this proof is included in Section 7.

We worked nearly a week before the system was able to do this proof. However, once the proof was completed, the effort necessary to enable the system to do the proof of the unification algorithm was minimal. The latter proof, though longer than this one, did not require much additional intellectual capacity on the part of the deductive system. We do not show that proof here because it is similar to the pattern matcher proof, but we include the program and the assertion we proved about it.

4.3. The Unification Algorithm

The problem of unification is similar to that of pattern matching except that we allow both arguments to contain variables. We expect the algorithm to find a substitution that makes the two arguments identical when it is applied to both, if such a substitution exists. For example, if x is (F U A) and y is (F B V), then $unify(x, y)$ is ((U·B) (V·A)), where U and V are variables and A, B, and F are constants.

A simple program to unify x and y is

```
unify(x, y) = prog((m1 m2)
    if x = y then return(EMPTY)
    if var(x) then
        return(if occursin(x, y)  then NOMATCH
                                  else list(cons(x, y)))
    if var(y) then
        return(if occursin(y, x)  then NOMATCH
                                  else list(cons(y, x)))
    if atom(x) then return(NOMATCH)
    if atom(y) then return(NOMATCH)
    m1 ← unify(car(x), car(y))
```

if $m1$ = NOMATCH then return (NOMATCH)
$m2 \leftarrow unify(varsubst(m1, cdr(x)),$
$\qquad\qquad\qquad varsubst(m1, cdr(y)))$
if $m2$ = NOMATCH then return(NOMATCH)
return($compose(m2, m1)$)).

The predicate $occursin(u, v)$ tests if u occurs in v. This program is a recursive, list-oriented version of Robinson's iterative, string-oriented program. Again, we have verified only the longest path of the program, not the entire program. Furthermore, we have proved not the strongest possible statement about this program, but only that

$unify(x,y) \neq$ NOMATCH $\supset$
$varsubst(unify(x, y), x) = varsubst(unify(x,y), y).$

4.4. The FIND Program

The program FIND, described by Hoare (1961), is intended to rearrange an array A so that all the elements to the left of a certain index F are less than or equal to A[F], and all those to the right of F are greater than or equal to A[F]. In other words, the relation (STRIP (BAGA A 1 F−1)) ⩽ A[F] ⩽ (STRIP (BAGA A F+1 NN)) should hold when the program halts. For instance, if F is NN÷2, then A[F] is the median of the array. The function is useful in computing percentiles and is fairly complex.

Hoare remarks that a sorting program would achieve the same purpose but would usually require much more time; the conditions for FIND are much weaker in that, for example, the elements to the left of F need not be sorted themselves, as long as none of them are greater than A[F].

The ALGOL representation of FIND is as follows:

```
FIND (F,NN,A); INTEGER F,NN; INTEGER ARRAY A[1:NN]
BEGIN
  INTEGER M,N;
  M ← 1;
  N ← NN;
  WHILE M < N DO
    BEGIN INTEGER R,I,J;
      R ← A[F];
      I ← M;
      J ← N;
      WHILE I ⩽ J DO
```

```
BEGIN WHILE A[I] < R DO I ← I+1 ;
WHILE R < A[J] DO J ← J−1 ;
IF I ≤ J THEN
BEGIN EXCHANGE (A I J);
  I ← I+1;
  J ← J−1
END
END
IF F ≤ J THEN N ← J
ELSE IF I ≤ F THEN M ← I
    ELSE GO TO L
END
 L:
END
```

The general strategy of the program FIND is to move "small" elements to the left and "large" elements to the right. These relative size categories are defined as being less than or not less than an arbitrary array element. The algorithm scans the array from left to right looking for a large element; when it finds one, it scans from right to left looking for a small element. When it finds one, it exchanges the large element and the small element it has already found, and the scan from the left continues where it left off until the next large element is found, and so on. When the scan from the left and the scan from the right meet somewhere in the middle, they define a split in the array. We can then show that all the elements to the left of the split are small and all those to the right are large.

The index F can be either to the left or to the right of the split, but suppose it is to the left. Then the elements to the right of the split can remain where they are; they are the largest elements in the array, and the element that will ultimately be in position F is to the left of the split. We then disregard the right portion of the array and repeat the process with the split as the upper bound of the array and with a refined definition of "large" and "small". We will eventually find a new split; suppose this split is to the left of F. We can then leave in place the elements of the array to the left of the split and work only with the elements to the right; we readjust the left bound of the array to occur at the split, and we repeat the process. Thus, the left and right bounds of the array move closer and closer together, but they always have F between them. Finally, they meet at F, and the algorithm halts.

The flowchart in Figure 1.6 follows Hoare's algorithm closely.

In this program, I is the pointer for the left-to-right scan, J is the pointer for the right-to-left scan, M and N are the lower and upper bounds of the "middle" portion of the array, and R is the value used to discriminate between small and large array elements. Hoare (1971) provided an informal manual proof of the correctness of his program. Deutsch (1973) and Igarashi, London, and Luckham (1975) have produced machine proofs. The proof we obtained required a minimal number (three) of intermediate assertions; however, one of the verification conditions produced was quite difficult to prove. This condition corresponds to the statement that the elements to the right of the right boundary dominate the elements to its left after an exchange is performed and a new right boundary is established. We present a sketch of this proof below.

4.4.1. Assertions for FIND

The input assertion q_s for FIND is (the conjunction of)

$$1 \leqslant F \leqslant NN,$$

$$A = AP,$$

The array AP is the initial version of A; we define it in the input assertion so that we can refer to it after we have modified A.

The output assertion q_H is

(STRIP (BAGA A 1 F−1)) ⩽ A[F] ⩽ (STRIP (BAGA A F+1 NN))
(BAGA A 1 NN) = (BAGA AP 1 NN).

The second conjunct of q_H states that when the program terminates, the array A is indeed a permutation of the initial array AP.

The intermediate assertion q_1 is

1 ⩽ M ⩽ F ⩽ N ⩽ NN
(STRIP (BAGA A 1 M−1)) ⩽ (STRIP (BAGA A M NN))
(STRIP (BAGA A 1 N)) ⩽ STRIP (BAGA A N+1 NN))
(BAGA A 1 NN) = (BAGA AP 1 NN).

This assertion is reached whenever a new bound on the middle section of the array is established.

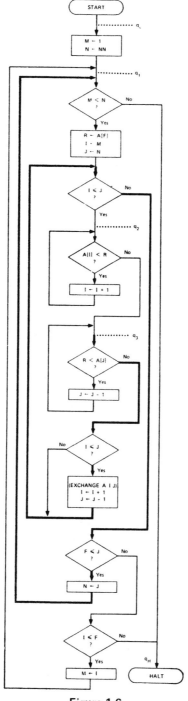

Figure 1.6.

The assertion q_2 is

$1 \leqslant M \leqslant F \leqslant N \leqslant NN$
(STRIP (BAGA A 1 M−1)) $\leqslant$ (STRIP (BAGA A M NN))
(STRIP (BAGA A 1 N)) $\leqslant$ (STRIP (BAGA A N+1 NN))
$M \leqslant I$
$J \leqslant N$
(STRIP (BAGA A 1 I−1)) $\leqslant R \leqslant$ (STRIP (BAGA A J+1 NN))
(BAGA A 1 NN) = (BAGA AP 1 NN).

The assertion q_3 is the same as the assertion q_2, with the additional conjunct

$$R \leqslant A[I].$$

4.4.2 The Proof

All but one of the verification conditions for this program were proved fairly easily. The one difficult condition corresponds to the path beginning at q_3 that follows the heavy line and finally ends at q_1. The verification-condition generator supplied us with the following hypotheses:

$1 \leqslant M \leqslant F \leqslant N \leqslant NN,$ $\hspace{3cm}$ (1.43)

(STRIP (BAGA A 1 M−1)) $\leqslant$ (STRIP (BAGA A M NN)), $\hspace{1cm}$ (1.44)

(STRIP (BAGA A 1 N)) $\leqslant$ (STRIP (BAGA A N+1 NN)), $\hspace{1cm}$ (1.45)

$M \leqslant I,$ $\hspace{7cm}$ (1.46)

$J \leqslant N,$ $\hspace{7cm}$ (1.47)

(STRIP (BAGA A 1 I−1)) $\leqslant R \leqslant$ (STRIP (BAGA A J+1 NN)), (1.48)

$R \leqslant A[I],$ $\hspace{6.5cm}$ (1.49)

(BAGA AP 1 NN) = (BAGA A 1 NN), $\hspace{2.5cm}$ (1.50)

$\neg(R < A[J]),$ $\hspace{6cm}$ (1.51)

$I \leqslant J,$ $\hspace{7cm}$ (1.52)

$\neg(I+1 \leqslant J−1),$ $\hspace{5cm}$ (1.53)

$F \leqslant J−1.$ $\hspace{6.5cm}$ (1.54)

The interesting consequence for this path is

(STRIP (BAGA A′ 1 J−1)) $\leqslant$ (STRIP (BAGA A′ (J−1)+1 NN)),

$$\hspace{8cm} (1.55)$$

where

$$A' = (EXCHANGE\ A\ I\ J),$$

the array that results when elements A[I] and A[J] are interchanged in A.

The proof sketched below roughly parallels the proof produced by the inference system. Portions of the trace are shown in Section 7.

The $(J-1)+1$ term in the goal (1.55) is simplified to J, giving the goal

$$(STRIP\ (BAGA\ A'\ 1\ J-1)) \leqslant (STRIP\ (BAGA\ A'\ J\ NN)). \qquad (1.56)$$

The difficulty in the proof arises from the uncertainty about whether $J \leqslant I$. We are reasoning about an array segment, and it is not clear whether that segment is affected by the exchange or not. Hand analysis of the hypotheses (1.52) and (1.53) reveals that I = J or I = J−1. The value of a term like (BAGA (EXCHANGE A I J) 1 J−1) depends on which possibility is actually the case.

The system "simplifies" the term into

```
(IF J ≤ I THEN (BAGA A 1 J−1)
         ELSE (BAG  (STRIP (BAGA A 1 I−1))
               A[J]
               (STRIP (BAGA A I+1 J−1))))).
```

Intuitively, if $J \leqslant I$, then both I and J are outside the bounds of the array segment, whereas if $I < J$, then the array segment loses A[I] but gains A[J].

Similarly, the term

$$(BAGA\ (EXCHANGE\ A\ I\ J)\ J\ NN)$$

is "simplified" into

```
(IF J ≤ I  THEN (BAGA A J NN)
         ELSE (BAG (STRIP (BAGA A J J−1))
               A[I]
               (STRIP (BAGA A J+1 NN))))).
```

Note that (BAGA A J J−1) is empty; the ELSE clause is then

$$(BAG\ A[I]\ (STRIP\ (BAGA\ A\ J+1\ NN))).$$

Our goal can thus be reduced to showing that

(IF J ≤ I THEN (STRIP (BAGA A 1 J−1))
       ELSE (STRIP (BAG (STRIP (BAGA A 1 I−1))
              A[J]
              (STRIP (BAGA A I+J J−1)))))

≤

(IF J ≤ I THEN (STRIP (BAGA A J NN))
       ELSE (STRIP (BAG A[I]
              (STRIP (BAGA A J+1 NN)))))).

$$(1.57)$$

The system approaches the conditional expression by creating two contexts: In one context, J ≤ I holds, and in the other, I < J. In the first context we must prove that

(STRIP (BAGA A 1 J−1)) ≤ (STRIP (BAGA A J NN)). $$(1.58)$$

In the second context, the statement to be proved is

(STRIP (BAG (STRIP (BAGA A 1 I−1))
           A[J]
           (STRIP (BAGA A I+1 J−1))))

≤

(STRIP (BAG A[I]
           (STRIP (BAGA A J+1 NN))))). $$(1.59)$$

Note that in the first context, J = I by (1.52). In working on (1.58), (BAGA A J NN) is expanded to (BAG A[J] (STRIP (BAGA A J+1 NN))). Thus, (1.58) breaks into two subgoals:

(STRIP (BAGA A 1 J−1)) ≤ A[J] $$(1.60)$$

and

(STRIP (BAGA A 1 J−1)) ≤ (STRIP (BAGA A J+1 NN)).

$$(1.61)$$

Since I = J, (1.60) follows from (1.48) and (1.49), and (1.61) follows from (1.48) alone.

Work on the goal (1.59) proceeds in the second context, in which I < J. Since J−1 < I+1 (1.53), we know (BAGA A I+1 J−1) is empty.

The inequality (1.59) may thus be broken into four inequalities:

$$(STRIP (BAGA A 1 I-1)) \leqslant A[I], \tag{1.62}$$

$$(STRIP (BAGA A 1 I-1)) \leqslant (STRIP (BAGA A J+1 NN)), \tag{1.63}$$

$$A[J] \leqslant A[I], \tag{1.64}$$

and

$$A[J] \leqslant (STRIP (BAGA A J+1 NN)). \tag{1.65}$$

The goal (1.62) follows from the hypotheses (1.48) and (1.49). The goal (1.63) follows from (1.48). The goal (1.64) follows from (1.49) and (1.51). The goal (1.65) follows from (1.51) and (1.48). This completes the proof.

This proof is the most complex achieved by our deductive system so far.

5. Conclusion

5.1 Summary of Results

Complete proofs have been found of the correctness of the following algorithms:

(1) Finding the largest element of an array.
(2) Finding the quotient of two real numbers.
(3) Hoare's FIND program.
(4) The Euclidean algorithm for finding the greatest common divisor.
(5) The exponentiation program from King's thesis.
(6) Integer quotient and remainder.
(7) Integer multiplication by repeated addition.
(8) Computing the factorial of a nonnegative integer.

Theorems have been proved about the following algorithms:

(1) The pattern matcher.
(2) Unification.

(3) Exchanging two array elements (the theorem is that the bag of the contents of the array is unchanged).

(4) King's exchange sort.

We believe the system now has the power to do all of King's problem set except the linear inequalities problem, which is not really a proof about an algorithm.

5.2. Future Plans

We are currently applying the verifier to more and more complex programs in a variety of subject domains. We are continuously being forced to add new rules and occasionally to generalize old ones; a special-purpose rule that worked for one problem may not work for the next.

The deductive system is implemented in the QA4 language. Although QA4 is ideally suited for expressing our rules, it is an experimental system evaluated by an interpreter which is written in LISP; furthermore, it uses space inefficiently. Reboh and Sacerdoti have integrated QA4 into INTERLISP to produce a system known as QLISP (Wilber, 1976). QLISP programs are translated into LISP programs that can be evaluated by the LISP interpreter or even compiled. Furthermore, QLIP is much more conservative in its use of space. The QLISP system is considerably faster and more compact that the QA4 system. Our deductive system has already been translated into QLISP, and the same proofs are carried out many times faster.

QA4 subtly encourages its users to write depth-first search strategies, since it implements the goal mechanism by means of backtracking. The deductive system uses depth-first search and, for the most part, this has been the proper thing to do. There have been times, however, when we have felt the need for something more discriminating. Suppose, for example, we are trying to prove an expression of the form $x = y$. We can do this by trying to simplify x and then proving that the simplified x is equal to y, or we can try to find some assertion $a = b$ and prove $x = a$ and $y = b$. In the current system, we must exhaust one possibility before trying another, whereas we would like to be able to switch back and forth between different approaches, giving more attention to the one that currently seems to be making the best progress. In other words, we hope to use processes rather than backtracking in the implementation of the goal mechanism.

Finally, we hope to apply this work to the generation of counterexamples for "wrong" programs, to the generation of Floyd assertions, and to the automatic construction of programs. It seems inevitable that if we know how to reason about programs, that reasoning should be able to help us in the process of forming or changing a program. Rather than taking a handwritten and hand-debugged program to a verifier for approval, we hope to collaborate with a system that will play an active role in the creation of the algorithm.

6. Appendix: Annotated Listing of the Deductive System

The deductive system has the overall structure shown in Figure 1.7. The names on the chart are either function names or goal classes. Only important substructures and relationships are included.

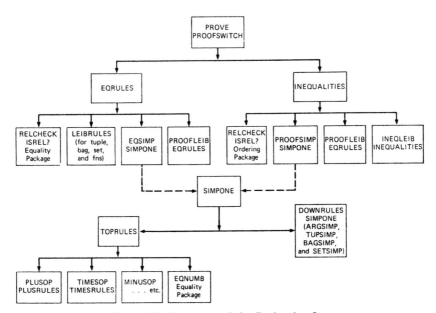

Figure 1.7. Structure of the Deductive System.

An annotated listing of the programs used for reasoning is presented below. An index of functions and goal classes is included at the end of this appendix. The reader will note how little of the space is devoted to general strategies and how much is devoted to subject-specific knowledge. Some of the programs use QA4 features that are not described in this paper. The reader can rely on the English explication of the programs, or he can refer to the QA4 manual (Rulifson et al., 1972).

To start a deduction, we say to the system

$$(GOAL \ \$PROVE \ \langle some \ statement\rangle)$$

- PROVE is a goal class: [4]

$$(TUPLE \ ANDSPLIT \ ORSPLIT \ ORSPLITMANY \ PROOFSWITCH)$$

- The rule ANDSPLIT takes a goal that is a conjunction of two or more expressions [5] and tries to prove each conjunct independently.

```
ANDSPLIT=(LAMBDA (AND ←X ←←Y)
                (ATTEMPT (GOAL $GOALCLASS $X)
                        THEN
                        (ATTEMPT (GOAL $GOALCLASS
                                         (AND $$Y))
                                 ELSE
                                 (FAIL))
                        ELSE
                        (FAIL]⁶⁻⁸
```

If repeated applications of ANDSPLIT are successful eventually, the goal (AND)

---

[4] Bullets are used to indicate the beginning of the description of a new function.

[5] Variables with double prefixes, "←←" or "$$." respectively match or evaluate to a sequence of terms rather than a single term. In the rule, for example, Y can be bound to a set of terms, including the empty set.

[6] The right bracket represents a string of right parentheses long enough to balance the expression.

[7] The ATTEMPT statement is a conditional expression that tests for failure rather than falsehood, and has the additional power to restrict and control the effects of backtracking. For instance, suppose an expression of the form (ATTEMPT P THEN Q ELSE R) is being evaluated. If the evaluation of P is completed successfully, then Q is evaluated. On the other hand, if the evaluation of P results in a failure, then R is evaluated. A failure in P cannot cause the ATTEMPT statement to fail. A failure in Q or R, however, will cause the ATTEMPT statement to fail as usual.

[8] The ANDSPLIT rule occurs in several goal classes. The variable GOALCLASS that occurs in ANDSPLIT is bound by the system to whatever goal class was in effect when ANDSPLIT was invoked. Thus, ANDSPLIT applies to each conjunct the same goal class that was applied to the entire conjunction.

will be generated. However, (AND) is an assertion in the data base, and so the rule will then succeed.

• ORSPLIT applies to a goal that is the disjunction of two expressions and works on each separately.

> ORSPLIT=(LAMBDA (OR ←X ←Y)
>   (ATTEMPT (GOAL $GOALCLASS $X)
>   ELSE
>   (GOAL $GOALCLASS $Y]

The expression x is attempted as a goal first; if this is successful, we are done. Otherwise, ORSPLIT works on y; if it is unsuccessful, then a failure is generated.

• ORSPLITMANY is similar to ORSPLIT, except that it takes as a goal the disjunction of three or more expressions:

> ORSPLITMANY =
>   (LAMBDA (OR ←X ←Y ←Z ←←W)
>   (ATTEMPT (GOAL $GOALCLASS $X)
>   ELSE
>   (GOAL $GOALCLASS (OR $Y $Z $$W)

The expression x is attempted first; if the proof is successful, the disjunction is true. Otherwise, the disjunction of the remaining expressions is established as a new goal. Continued failure to prove members of a disjunction will eventually cause ORSPLIT to be invoked.

• PROOFSWITCH attempts to apply the appropriate goal class to prove a goal. It determines whether the goal is an equality; if not, it is assumed to be an inequality. (Other goal classes could be added with little difficulty.) If the proof is successful, the goal is added to the data base as an assertion.

> PROOFSWITCH=
>   (LAMBDA (←F ←X)
>   (PROG (DECLARE)
>   (IF (EQUAL $F (QUOTE EQ))
>   THEN
>   (GOAL $EQRULES ($F $X))
>   ELSE
>   (GOAL $INEQUALITIES ($F $X)))
>   (ASSERT ($F $X))
>   (RETURN ($F $X]

In either case, the appropriate set of rules is applied.

6.1. Equalities

• The equality class is

EQRULES =
(TUPLE ANDSPLIT ORSPLIT ORSPLITMANY RELCHECK EQTIMESDIVIDE
    EQSUBST LEIBT LEIBF LEIBB LEIBS EQSIMP PROOFLEIB)

• The rule RELCHECK merely checks the property lists of the expressions to
see if they are already known to be equal:

RELCHECK=(LAMBDA ←X (ISREL? $X]

When RELCHECK is applied, x is bound to an equality statement, which is fed
to the ISREL? statement. ISREL? will succeed not only if the equality has been
explicitly asserted, but also if the equality follows by the transitive law from
other equalities or inequalities. ISREL? is the mechanism for making queries
about special relations. It will work with inequality relations, such as LT, GTQ,
and NEQ, as well as EQ.
    EQTIMESDIVIDE and EQSUBST are rules for reasoning about numbers and
substitutions, respectively. They are discussed in the relevant sections.

• To prove $f(x) = f(y)$, try to prove $x = y$: this form of Leibniz's law for function applications is expressed by the rule LEIBF. The analogous rules for tuples,
sets, and bags are expressed by LEIBT, LEIBS, and LEIBB respectively.

```
LEIBF=(LAMBDA (EQ (←F ←X)
                  (←F ←Y))
        (PROG (DECLARE)
            ($ASK ('(EQ $X $Y))
                    PROVE?)
            (GOAL $EQRULES (EQ $X $Y]

LEIBT=(LAMBDA (EQ (TUPLE ←X ←←Z)
                  (TUPLE ←Y ←←W))
        (PROG (DECLARE)
            (GOAL $EQRULES (EQ $X $Y))
            (GOAL $EQRULES (EQ $Z $W]

LEIBS=(LAMBDA (EQ (SET ← X ←←Z)
                  (SET ←Y ←←Z))
        (GOAL $EQRULES (EQ $X $Y]

LEIBB=(LAMBDA (EQ (BAG ←X ←←Z)
                  (BAG ←Y ←←Z))
        (GOAL $EQRULES (EQ $X $Y]
```

L is expected to be LT or LTQ. To prove $x{<}y$, for example, find an asserted statement LOWER $<$ UPPER and prove $x{\leqslant}$LOWER and UPPER${\leqslant}y$.

- INEQIFTHENELSE is a rule that sets up a case analysis:

```
INEQIFTHENELSE=(LAMBDA
        (←F ←←W1 (IFTHENELSE ←X ←Y ←Z) ←←W2)
        (PROG (DECLARE VERICON)
            (ATTEMPT (SETQ ←VERICON
                            (CONTEXT PUSH LOCAL))
                (ASSERT $X WRT $VERICON)
                THEN
                (GOAL $INEQUALITIES
                    ($F $$W1 $Y $$W2)
                    WRT $VERICON))
            (ATTEMPT (SETQ ←VERICON
                            (CONTEXT PUSH LOCAL))
                (DENY $X WRT $VERICON)
                THEN
                (GOAL $INEQUALITIES
                    ($F $$W1 $Z $$W2)
                    WRT $VERICON)
            ELSE
            (RETURN (SUCCESS WITH
                        INEQIFTHENELSE]
```

For example, suppose the goal is (IF x THEN y ELSE z) $\leqslant w$. This rule establishes two subcontexts of the local context. In one of these contexts, x is true; in the other, x is false. In the first context, the rule tries to prove $y \leqslant w$, whereas in the second, it tries to prove $z \leqslant w$. Note that the subsystem that stores equalities and inequalities will cause a failure if an assertion (or a denial) would lead it to contradict what it knows. In that case the goal is considered to be achieved.

- INEQSTRIPBAG is an inequality rule that has a bag as one of its arguments.

```
INEQSTRIPBAG=(LAMBDA (←F ←←W (STRIP (BAG ←X ←←Y))
                        ←←Z)
                (GOAL $INEQUALITIES
                    (AND ($F $$W $X $$Z)
                        ($F $$W (STRIP (BAG $$Y))
                        $$Z ]
```

This rule would be invoked when we want to show, e.g., $w_1 \leqslant$ (STRIP (BAG c_1 c_2, ...)) $\leqslant w_2$. The intention here is to demonstrate that $w_1 \leqslant c_1 \leqslant w_2$ and $w_1 \leqslant c_2 \leqslant w_2$, and so forth. Ultimately, we might have to demonstrate that $w_1 \leqslant$(STRIP (BAG)) $\leqslant w_2$. The special relations handler (ISREL?)

succeeds vacuously with any inequality relation where one of the arguments is
(STRIP (BAG)).

6.3. Deduce

- DEDUCE is a goal class of rules that are guaranteed to terminate quickly. It is
used when we want something more inquisitive than EXISTS but less time-
consuming than PROVE, EQRULES, or INEQUALITIES.

```
DEDUCE=
(TUPLE RELCHECK ANDSPLIT ORSPLIT ORSPLITMANY LTPLUS
        FSUBTRACT1 FSUBTRACT2 LTQPLUS NOTATOM CONSTCAR
        CONSTCDR)
```

We have already described RELCHECK, ANDSPLIT, ORSPLIT, and ORSPLIT-
MANY.

The other DEDUCE rules are for special applications and are discussed in the
appropriate sections.

6.4. Simplification

- The top-level simplification function is SIMPONE. This function does not try
to simplify its argument completely. It will find a partial simplification; repeated
applications, if necessary, will completely simplify the expression.

The simplification rules may, of course, be added by the user. We expect that
each simplification rule should make the expression simpler in some sense.
Otherwise, the program may loop interminably.

```
SIMPONE=(LAMBDA ←GOAL1 (PROG
            (DECLARE SIMPGOAL)
            (IF (EQUAL (STYPE $GOAL1) NUMBER)
                THEN
                (FAIL))
            ($ASK $GOAL1 SIMPLIFY?)
            (SETQ ←SIMPGOAL
                (ATTEMPT
                    (GOAL $TOPRULES $GOAL1)
                    ELSE
                    ($TRY $TOPRULES
                        (GOAL $DOWNRULES $GOAL1))))
            (PUT $GOAL1 SIMPLIFIED $SIMPGOAL
                WRT ETERNAL)
            (RETURN $SIMPGOAL]
```

SIMPONE fails if it cannot simplify its argument at all. It treats numbers as

The LEIBF rule asks the user if he wants that rule to be applied. The function ASK that performs the interaction is described in the section on utility functions.

• EQSIMP and PROOFLEIB are very time-consuming but also very powerful. EQSIMP says: to prove $x = y$, simplify x and try to prove that the simplified x is equal to y.

```
EQSIMP=(LAMBDA (EQ ←X ←Y)
            (PROG (DECLARE)
                 (SETQ ←X ($SIMPONE $X))
                 (GOAL $EQRULES (EQ $X $Y)))
            (BACKTRACK]
```

Since the program uses the BACKTRACK option, and since EQ implicitly takes a set as its argument, EQSIMP can work on y as well as on x. In other words, if it fails to simplify x, it will go ahead and try to simplify y.

• PROOFLEIB tries to make use of information stored in the data base. It is used to prove inequalities as well as equalities.

```
PROOFLEIB=(LAMBDA (←F ←X)
                (PROG (DECLARE)
                     (EXISTS ($F ←Y))
                     ($ASK (' (EQ $X $Y))
                          PROVE?)
                     (GOAL $EQRULES (EQ $X $Y]
```

It says: to prove $u = v$, find an assertion of the form $a = b$ and prove $u = a$ and $v = b$. The rule relies on user interaction to cut off bad paths. Note that if f is EQ, we can expect x and y to be sets, so that LEIBS will ultimately be called to prove the equality expression generated by PROOFLEIB.

The EXISTS statement searches the data base for an assertion that matches its argument, binding the ← variables appropriately. Subsequent failure causes it to look for another matching assertion. When no more assertions match, the EXISTS statement itself fails.

6.2. Inequalities

We now turn to the rules for proving inequalities.

```
INEQUALITIES=
(TUPLE ANDSPLIT RELCHECK ORSPLIT ORSPLITMANY PROOFSIMP
        INEQIFTHENELSE INEQSTRIPBAG INEQSTRIPSTRIP
        INEQSTRIPTRAN GTQLTQ LTQMANY FSUBSTRACT1
        FSUBTRACT2 INEQTIMESDIVIDE EQINEQMONOTONE LTQPLUS
        PROOFLEIB INEQLEIB)
```

RELCHECK has been mentioned above.

- GTQLTQ says: to prove $y \geqslant x$, try to prove $x \leqslant y$:

$$\text{GTQLTQ} = (\text{LAMBDA (GTQ} \leftarrow\text{Y} \leftarrow\text{X)}$$
$$\text{(GOAL \$INEQUALITIES (LTQ \$X \$Y]}$$

- LTQMANY takes an inequality goal, such as

$$x_1 \leqslant x_2 \leqslant \cdots \leqslant x_n,$$

and breaks it into separate goals,

$$x_1 \leqslant x_2 \quad \text{and} \quad x_2 \leqslant x_3 \quad \text{and} \quad \cdots \quad \text{and} \quad x_{n-1} \leqslant x_n.$$

```
LTQMANY=(LAMBDA (LTQ ←X ←Y ←Z ←←W)
            (PROG (DECLARE)
                (GOAL $INEQUALITIES (LTQ $X $Y))
                (GOAL $INEQUALITIES
                    (LTQ $Y $Z $$W]
```

LTQPLUS, FSUBTRACT1, and FSUBTRACT2 are special rules for reasoning about numbers and are discussed in the relevant section.

- PROOFSIMP proves an expression $f(y)$ by trying to simplify y and proving the simplified expression.

```
PROOFSIMP=(LAMBDA (PAND ←X (←F ←Y))
              (PROG (DECLARE GOALCLASS1)
                  (SETQ ←GOALCLASS1 $GOALCLASS)
                  (ATTEMPT (SETQ ←X ($ARGSIMP $X))
                      ELSE
                      (FAIL))
                  (GOAL $GOALCLASS1 $X]
```

It has more general application than just to inequalities, although so far we have used it only for inequalities.

- INEQLEIB is similar to PROOFLEIB, but it works only for inequalities.

```
INEQLEIB=(LAMBDA (←L ←X ←Y)
             (PROG (DECLARE LOWER UPPER)
                 (EXISTS ($L ←LOWER ←UPPER))
                 ($ASK PROVE (' (LTQ $X $LOWER))
                     AND
                     (' (LTQ $UPPER $Y))
                     ?)
                 (GOAL $INEQUALITIES
                     (AND (LTQ $X $LOWER)
                         (LTQ $UPPER $Y]
```

L is expected to be LT or LTQ. To prove $x < y$, for example, find an asserted statement LOWER $<$ UPPER and prove $x \leqslant$ LOWER and UPPER$\leqslant y$.

- INEQIFTHENELSE is a rule that sets up a case analysis:

```
INEQIFTHENELSE=(LAMBDA
        (←F ←←W1 (IFTHENELSE ←X ←Y ←Z) ←←W2)
        (PROG (DECLARE VERICON)
            (ATTEMPT (SETQ ←VERICON
                            (CONTEXT PUSH LOCAL))
                (ASSERT $X WRT $VERICON)
                THEN
                (GOAL $INEQUALITIES
                    ($F $$W1 $Y $$W2)
                    WRT $VERICON))
            (ATTEMPT (SETQ ←VERICON
                            (CONTEXT PUSH LOCAL))
                (DENY $X WRT $VERICON)
                THEN
                (GOAL $INEQUALITIES
                    ($F $$W1 $Z $$W2)
                    WRT $VERICON)
            ELSE
            (RETURN (SUCCESS WITH
                    INEQIFTHENELSE]
```

For example, suppose the goal is (IF x THEN y ELSE z) $\leqslant w$. This rule establishes two subcontexts of the local context. In one of these contexts, x is true; in the other, x is false. In the first context, the rule tries to prove $y \leqslant w$, whereas in the second, it tries to prove $z \leqslant w$. Note that the subsystem that stores equalities and inequalities will cause a failure if an assertion (or a denial) would lead it to contradict what it knows. In that case the goal is considered to be achieved.

- INEQSTRIPBAG is an inequality rule that has a bag as one of its arguments.

```
INEQSTRIPBAG=(LAMBDA (←F ←←W (STRIP (BAG ←X ←←Y))
                        ←←Z)
                (GOAL $INEQUALITIES
                    (AND ($F $$W $X $$Z)
                        ($F $$W (STRIP (BAG $$Y))
                        $$Z ]
```

This rule would be invoked when we want to show, e.g., $w_1 \leqslant$ (STRIP (BAG c_1 c_2, ...)) $\leqslant w_2$. The intention here is to demonstrate that $w_1 \leqslant c_1 \leqslant w_2$ and $w_1 \leqslant c_2 \leqslant w_2$, and so forth. Ultimately, we might have to demonstrate that $w_1 \leqslant$ (STRIP (BAG)) $\leqslant w_2$. The special relations handler (ISREL?)

succeeds vacuously with any inequality relation where one of the arguments is
(STRIP (BAG)).

6.3. Deduce

• DEDUCE is a goal class of rules that are guaranteed to terminate quickly. It is
used when we want something more inquisitive than EXISTS but less time-
consuming than PROVE, EQRULES, or INEQUALITIES.

```
DEDUCE=
(TUPLE RELCHECK ANDSPLIT ORSPLIT ORSPLITMANY LTPLUS
        FSUBTRACT1 FSUBTRACT2 LTQPLUS NOTATOM CONSTCAR
        CONSTCDR)
```

We have already described RELCHECK, ANDSPLIT, ORSPLIT, and ORSPLIT-
MANY.

The other DEDUCE rules are for special applications and are discussed in the
appropriate sections.

6.4. Simplification

• The top-level simplification function is SIMPONE. This function does not try
to simplify its argument completely. It will find a partial simplification; repeated
applications, if necessary, will completely simplify the expression.

The simplification rules may, of course, be added by the user. We expect that
each simplification rule should make the expression simpler in some sense.
Otherwise, the program may loop interminably.

```
SIMPONE=(LAMBDA ←GOAL1 (PROG
            (DECLARE SIMPGOAL)
            (IF (EQUAL (STYPE $GOAL1) NUMBER)
                THEN
                (FAIL))
            ($ASK $GOAL1 SIMPLIFY?)
            (SETQ ←SIMPGOAL
                (ATTEMPT
                    (GOAL $TOPRULES $GOAL1)
                    ELSE
                    ($TRY $TOPRULES
                        (GOAL $DOWNRULES $GOAL1)))))
            (PUT $GOAL1 SIMPLIFIED $SIMPGOAL
                WRT ETERNAL)
            (RETURN $SIMPGOAL]
```

SIMPONE fails if it cannot simplify its argument at all. It treats numbers as being completely simplified. It asks the user for permission to go ahead. It tries a goal class, TOPRULES, on the expression.

- TOPRULES is a set of rules that work on the top level of the expression:

TOPRULES =
(TUPLE HASSIMP FAILINTODOWNRULES PLUSOP TIMESOP MINUSOP
        FIFTHENELSE BAGAOP SUBSTOP EXPZERO EXPEXP SUBPLUS
        SUBNUM GCDEQ ACCH CONSDIFF DIFDIF DIFFCONS DIFFONE
        MAXPLUS MAXONE BAGSTRIP ACCEX EQNUMB)

If any of these rules apply, SIMPONE returns the simplified expression as its value. Otherwise, it tries to simplify some subexpression of the given expression:

DOWNRULES=(TUPLE ARGSIMP TUPSIMP BAGSIMP SETSIMP)

ARGSIMP=(LAMBDA (←F ←X)
                    (SUBST ('($F $X))
                            (TUPLE $X ($SIMPONE $X]

TUPSIMP=(LAMBDA (TUPLE ←←X ←Y ←←Z)
                    (TUPLE $$X ($SIMPONE $Y)
                          $$Z)
                    BACKTRACK]

BAGSIMP=(LAMBDA (BAG ←X ←←Y)
                    (BAG ($SIMPONE $X)
                          $$Y)
                    BACKTRACK]

SETSIMP=(LAMBDA (SET ←X ←←Y)
                    (SET ($SIMPONE $X)
                          $$Y)
                    BACKTRACK]

The DOWNRULES simplify a complex expression by simplifying the component parts of the expression. If any of the DOWNRULES applies, SIMPONE applies the TOPRULES again to the new expression. SIMPONE calls the functions ASK and TRY that are described in the section on utility functions.

- SIMPONE puts the simplified expression on the property list of the original expression. In this way, if it ever comes across the original expression again, one of the TOPRULES, HASSIMP, will immediately know what simplification was found before.

HASSIMP=(LAMBDA ←X (IF (NOT (IN (SETQ ←X (GET $X SIMPLIFIED))
                                (TUPLE DONE NOSUCHPROPERTY)))
                    THEN $X ELSE (FAIL]

• If the expression to be simplified is a set, tuple, or bag rather than a function application, none of the TOPRULES will apply to it. To avoid the cost of searching for a match among all the TOPRULES, the rule FAILINTODOWN-RULES will first test for this condition and cause the entire goal statement to fail should it arise:

```
FAILINTODOWNRULES=(LAMBDA ←X
                    (IF (IN (STYPE $X)
                           (TUPLE TUPLE SET BAG))
                    THEN
                    (FAIL GOAL)
                    ELSE
                    (FAIL]
```

SIMPONE will then apply the DOWNRULES to the argument to see if any of its subexpressions can be simplified.

• One of the most general TOPRULES is EQNUMB, which replaces any expression by the "smallest" known equal expression:

```
EQNUMB=(LAMBDA ←X (PROG (DECLARE BEST EQSET)
                  (IF (EQUAL (SETQ ←EQSET (GET $X EQ))
                            NOSUCHPROPERTY)
                  THEN
                  (FAIL))
                  (SETQ ←BEST ($SHORTEST $EQSET))
                  (IF (EQUAL $BEST $X)
                  THEN
                  (FAIL)
                  ELSE
                  (RETURN $BEST]
```

The "smallest" element of a set is computed by the QA4 function SHORTEST, described among the utility functions. If EQNUMB fails to find a smaller representation for x, it fails.

• FIFTHENELSE=(LAMBDA (←F (IFTHENELSE ←W ←X ←Y))
                    ('(IFTHENELSE $W ($F $X)
                                    ($F $Y])

FIFTHENELSE moves conditional expressions outside of function applications. An expression of the form

$$f(\text{IF } w \text{ THEN } x \text{ ELSE } y)$$

translates into

$$\text{IF } w \text{ THEN } f(x) \text{ ELSE } f(y).$$

The remaining rules in TOPRULES are discussed in the sections dealing with special subject domains.

6.5. Reasoning About Numbers

6.5.1. Equality and inequality rules

• EQTIMESDIVIDE is an EQRULE. It means that to prove $w = (x/y)*z$, one should prove $w*y = x*z$:

```
EQTIMESDIVIDE=(LAMBDA (EQ ←W (TIMES (DIVIDE ←X ←Y)
                                     ←←Z))
              (GOAL $EQRULES (EQ (TIMES $Y $W)
                                 (TIMES $X $$Z)))
              BACKTRACK]
```

Some inequality rules that know about numbers are presented below.

• LTQPLUS says that to prove $i \leqslant j+k$, one should prove $i \leqslant j$ and $0 \leqslant k$:

```
LTQPLUS=(LAMBDA (LTQ ←I (PLUS ←J ←K))
        (GOAL $DEDUCE (AND (LTQ $I $J)
                           (LTQ 0 $K)))
        BACKTRACK]
```

First, the rule attempts to prove that $i \leqslant j$ and $0 \leqslant k$. If either of these proofs is unsuccessful, then the backtracking mechanism will interchange the bindings of the arguments of LTQPLUS. This then leads to an attempt to prove $i \leqslant k$ and $0 \leqslant j$.

• LTPLUS is the analogue of LTQPLUS for LT:

```
LTPLUS=(LAMBDA (LT ←I (PLUS ←J ←K))
       (GOAL $DEDUCE (AND (LTQ $I $J)
                          (LT 0 $K)))
       BACKTRACK]
```

It means: to prove $i < j+k$, prove $i \leqslant j$ and $0 < k$. It can backtrack to reverse the roles of j and k.

• FSUBTRACT1 and FSUBTRACT2 allow us to remove subtraction from the goal; for example, to prove $x-y \leqslant z$, try to prove $x \leqslant y+z$.

```
FSUBTRACT1=(LAMBDA (←F (SUBTRACT ←X ←Y)
                       ←Z)
           (GOAL $GOALCLASS ($F $X (PLUS $Y $Z]
```

FSUBTRACT2=(LAMBDA (←F ←X (SUBTRACT ←Y ←Z))
                    (GOAL $GOALCLASS ($F (PLUS $X $Z)
                                            $Y]

- EQINEQMONOTONE says: to prove $w+x \leqslant y+z$, prove $w \leqslant y$ and $x \leqslant z$ or $w \leqslant z$ and $x \leqslant y$.

EQINEQMONOTONE=(LAMBDA (←L (PLUS ←W ←X)
                            (PLUS ←Y ←Z))
                        (PROG (DECLARE)
                            ($ASK PROVE ('($L $W $Y))
                                AND
                                ('($L $X $Z))
                                ?)
                            (GOAL $GOALCLASS
                                (AND ($L $W $Y)
                                      ($L $X $Z]
                    BACKTRACK]

- The rule INEQTIMESDIVIDE is similar to EQTIMESDIVIDE except that it must check that the denominator is nonnegative before multiplying out:

INEQTIMESDIVIDE=(LAMBDA (←F ←W (TIMES (DIVIDE ←X ←Y)
                                          ←←Z))
                        (PROG (DECLARE)
                            (GOAL $DEDUCE (LT 0 $Y))
                            (GOAL $INEQUALITIES
                                ($F (TIMES $Y $W)
                                      (TIMES $X $$Z))))
                    BACKTRACK]

This rule says: to prove $w < (x/y)^*z$, say, in the case that $0 < y$, try to prove $w^*y < x^*z$.

6.5.2. Numerical demons

- When $x \geqslant y$ is asserted, assert that $y \leqslant x$:

(WHEN EXP (GTQ ←X ←Y)
        INDICATOR MODELVALUE THEN (ASSERT (LTQ $Y $X)
                                          WRT $VERICON]

These demons make their assertions with respect to the current context, VERICON.

- Whenever $x+y \leqslant x+z$ is asserted, we want to conclude that $y \leqslant z$:

(WHEN EXP (LTQ (PLUS ←X ←Y)
                (PLUS ←X ←Z))
        INDICATOR MODELVALUE THEN
            (ASSERT (LTQ $Y $Z)
                    WRT $VERICON]

- Whenever $w-x \leqslant y$ is asserted, assert $w \leqslant x+y$, simplifying the right side if possible.

```
(WHEN EXP (LTQ (SUBTRACT ←W ←X)
              ←Y)
      INDICATOR MODELVALUE THEN
      (PROG (DECLARE RTSIDE)
            (SETQ ←RTSIDE
                  ($TRYALL $PLUSRULES
                           (' (PLUS $Y $X]
            (ASSERT (LTQ $W $RTSIDE)
                    WRT $VERICON))))
```

- Whenever $(w-x)+x \leqslant y$ is asserted, then assert $w \leqslant y$:

```
WHEN EXP (LTQ (PLUS (SUBTRACT ←W ←X)
                    ←X)
              ←Y)
     INDICATOR MODELVALUE THEN
     (ASSERT (LTQ $W $Y)
             WRT $VERICON]
```

Certain demons are intended exclusively for the integer domain.

- $x < y \supset x+1 \leqslant y$:

```
(WHEN EXP (LT ←X ←Y)
      INDICATOR MODELVALUE THEN
      (ASSERT (LTQ (PLUS $X 1)
                   $Y)
              WRT $VERICON]
```

- $x > y \supset y+1 \leqslant x$:

```
(WHEN EXP (GT ←X ←Y)
      INDICATOR MODELVALUE THEN
      (ASSERT (LTQ (PLUS $Y 1)
                   $X)
              WRT $VERICON]
```

Whenever $w-x < y$ is denied, *deny* $w \leqslant y+x-1$, simplifying if possible:

```
(WHEN EXP (LT (SUBTRACT ←W ←X)
             ←Y)
      INDICATOR MODELVALUE PUTS FALSE THEN
      (PROG (DECLARE RTSIDE)
            (SETQ
             ←RTSIDE
```

$$(\$TRYALL \; \$PLUSRULES$$
$$('(PLUS \; \$Y \; \$X$$
$$(MINUS \; 1))))$$
$$(DENY \; (LTQ \; \$W \; \$RTSIDE)$$
$$WRT \; \$VERICON]$$

6.5.3. Numerical simplification

Much of the knowledge the system has about numbers is embedded in the simplifier. For efficiency, these rules have been arranged hierarchically. For example, only one rule, PLUSOP, in TOPRULES deals with sums.[9]

$$PLUSOP=(LAMBDA \; (PAND \leftarrow Y \; (PLUS \; \leftarrow\leftarrow X))$$
$$(\$TRYALLFAIL \; \$PLUSRULES \; \$Y]$$

However, this one rule coordinates a multitude of other rules. All the rules that operate on plus expressions are in the goal class PLUSRULES.

$$PLUSRULES=(TUPLE \; PLUSEMPTY \; PLUSSINGLE \; PLUSZERO \; PLUSPLUS$$
$$PLUSMINUS \; PLUSDIFFERENCE \; PLUSCOMBINE$$
$$PLUSNUMBER)$$

The strategy PLUSOP uses is to apply all the PLUSRULES to its argument until no further simplification is possible. (The function TRYALLFAIL, that expresses this strategy, is described among the utility functions.) If PLUSOP can find no simplification at all, it fails.

Most of the PLUSRULES are quite simple.

• The sum of the empty bag is 0:

$$PLUSEMPTY=(LAMBDA \; (PLUS) \; 0)$$

• The sum of a bag of one element is that element itself:

$$PLUSSINGLE=(LAMBDA \; (PLUS \; \leftarrow X) \; \$X]$$

(i.e., $+x = x$).
• $x+0 = +x$:

$$PLUSZERO=(LAMBDA \; (PLUS \; \leftarrow\leftarrow X \; 0) \; (' \; (PLUS \; \$\$X]$$

---

[9] A pattern (PAND *pat*1 *pat*2) will match an argument if and only if *pat*1 and *pat*2 both match that argument.

Note that this rule implicitly says

$$0 + x = +x,$$

$$x + 0 + y = x + y,$$

$$x + y + 0 + z = x + y + z,$$

and so forth, because PLUS takes a bag as its argument.

● $((x_1+x_2+...)+y_1+y_2+...) = (x_1+x_2+...+y_1+y_2+...)$:

> PLUSPLUS=(LAMBDA (PLUS (PLUS ←←X) ←←Y)
>   (' (PLUS $$X $$Y]

● $x+(-x)+y = +y$:

> PLUSMINUS=(LAMBDA (PLUS ←X (MINUS ←X) ←←Y)
>   (' (PLUS $$Y]

● $x+(y-z)+w = x+y+w+(-z)$:

> PLUSDIFFERENCE=(LAMBDA (PLUS ←X (SUBTRACT ←Y ←Z) ←←W)
>   ($TRY (TUPLE PLUSMINUS)
>   (' (PLUS $Y $X $$W (MINUS $Z]

Note that **PLUSDIFFERENCE** recommends that **PLUSMINUS** be attempted immediately afterward. This is merely advice; if PLUSMINUS does not apply, nothing is lost. (**TRY** is described in the section on utility functions.)

● $x+x+y = 2*x+y$:

> PLUSCOMBINE=(LAMBDA (PLUS ←X ←X ←←Y)
>   ($TRYSUB $TIMESRULES ON
>   (' (TIMES 2 $X))
>   IN
>   (' (PLUS (TIMES 2 $X) $$Y]

Note that **PLUSCOMBINE** recommends that the $2*x$ term be simplified if possible. (**TRYSUB** is explained in the section on utility functions.)

● If two elements of a plus expression are syntactically numbers, **PLUS-NUMBER** will add them up:

> PLUSNUMBER=(LAMBDA (PLUS ←X ←Y ←←Z)
>   (PROG (DECLARE SUM)

```
                            ($INSIST (EQUAL (STYPE $X)
                                            NUMBER))
                            ($INSIST (EQUAL (STYPE $Y)
                                            NUMBER))
                            (SETQ ←SUM (PLUS $X $Y))
                            (RETURN (PLUS $SUM $$Z)))
                   BACKTRACK]
```

- The rule TIMESOP is strategically similar to PLUSOP:

$$\text{TIMESOP=(LAMBDA (PAND ←Y (TIMES ←←X))}$$
$$\text{($TRYALLFAIL $TIMESRULES $Y]}$$

It will apply all the TIMESRULES to the expression in question. TIMESRULES is

```
TIMESRULES =
(TUPLE TIMESEMPTY TIMESSINGLE TIMESZERO TIMESONE TIMESPLUS
       TIMESTIMES CANCEL SQRULE TIMESEXP TIMESDIVIDEONE)
```

- The product of the empty bag is 1:

$$\text{TIMESEMPTY=(LAMBDA (TIMES) 1)}$$

- The product of a bag of one element is that element itself:

$$\text{TIMESSINGLE=(LAMBDA (TIMES ←X) $X)}$$

- $0*y = 0$:

$$\text{TIMESZERO=(LAMBDA (TIMES 0 ←←Y) 0)}$$

- $1*x = x$:

$$\text{TIMESONE=(LAMBDA (TIMES 1 ←←X)}$$
$$\text{(' (TIMES $$X]}$$

Recall that these rules also imply

$$x*1*y = x*y,$$

$$x*0*y*z = 0,$$

and so forth.

- $(x+y)*z = x*z+(+y)*z$ (distributive law), where $+y$ represents a sum of one or more terms:

TIMESPLUS=(LAMBDA (TIMES (PLUS ←X ←←Y) ←←Z)
(\$TRY \$PLUSRULES (\$TRYSUB \$PLUSRULES ON ('(PLUS \$\$Y))
                    IN
                    ('(PLUS (TIMES \$X \$\$Z)
                           (TIMES (PLUS \$\$Y) \$\$Z]

(Some simplification is attempted immediately on $+y$ and on $x*z + (+y)*z$.
TRYSUB is explained in the section on utility functions.)

- $((x_1*x_2*...)*y_1*y_2...) = (x_1*x_2*...*y_1*y_2*...)$:

            TIMESTIMES=(LAMBDA (TIMES (TIMES ←←X) ←←Y)
                        ('(TIMES \$\$X \$\$Y]

- $x*(1/y)*z = (x/y)*z$:

        TIMESDIVIDEONE=(LAMBDA (TIMES ←X (DIVIDE 1 ←Y) ←←Z)
                        ('(TIMES (DIVIDE \$X \$Y)
                                \$\$Z]

- $x*(y/x)*z = y*z$:

        CANCEL=(LAMBDA (TIMES ←X (DIVIDE←Y ←X) ←←Z)
                ('(TIMES \$Y \$\$Z]

- $x*x*y = x^2*y$:

        SQRULE=(LAMBDA (TIMES ←X ←X ←←Y)
                (\$TRY (TUPLE TIMESSINGLE)
                ('(TIMES (EXP \$X 2) \$\$Y]

- $x*x^n*y = x^{n+1}*y$:

        TIMESEXP=(LAMBDA (TIMES ←X (EXP ←X ←N) ←←Y)
                (\$TRYSUB \$PLUSRULES ON ('(PLUS \$N 1))
                    IN
                    ('(TIMES (EXP \$X (PLUS \$N 1)) \$\$Y]

- To the reader who has gotten this far, MINUSOP will be self-explanatory:

MINUSOP=
(LAMBDA (MINUS ←X)
        (GOAL (TUPLE MINUSZERO MINUSMINUS MINUSPLUS)
        (MINUS \$X]

Note that MINUSOP, unlike PLUSOP and TIMESOP, does not apply *all* the rules to the expression, but will return the value of the first rule that does not fail.

- $-0 = 0$:

MINUSZERO=(LAMBDA (MINUS 0) 0)

- $-(-x) = x$:

MINUSMINUS=(LAMBDA (MINUS (MINUS ←X)) $X)

- $-(x+y) = (-x)+(-y)$:

MINUSPLUS=(LAMBDA (MINUS (PLUS ←X ←←Y))
          ($TRY $PLUSRULES (PLUS (MINUS $X)
                                 (MINUS (PLUS $$Y]

At present there are only two subtraction rules, and so we do not combine them into one operator:

- $x-y = x+(-y)$:

SUBPLUS=(LAMBDA (SUBSTRACT ←X ←Y)
        ($TRY $PLUSRULES (' (PLUS $X (MINUS $Y]

- If x and y are both numbers and not variables, SUBNUM actually evaluates $x-y$:

SUBNUM=LAMBDA (SUBTRACT ←X ←Y)
       (PROG (DECLARE)
             ($INSIST (AND (EQUAL (STYPE $X) NUMBER)
                           (EQUAL (STYPE $Y)
                                  NUMBER)))
             (RETURN (= (SUBTRACT $X $Y]

The "=" sign forces the system to evaluate what it would otherwise merely instantiate. INSIST is another utility function. Two more rules about exponentiation are given below.

- $x^0 = 1$:

EXPZERO=(LAMBDA (EXP ←X 0) 1)

- $(x^y)^z = x^{y*z}$:

EXPEXP=(LAMBDA (EXP (EXP ←X ←Y) ←Z)
       ($TRYSUB $TIMESRULE ON (' (TIMES $Y $Z))
                IN
                (' (EXP $X (TIMES $Y $Z]

Note that EXPEXP recommends that the TIMESRULES be applied to the product $y*z$; this is heuristic advice that could have been omitted.

- $gcd(x\ x) = x$:

        GCDEQ=(LAMBDA (GCD ←X ←Y)
                (PROG (DECLARE)
                     (GOAL $DEDUCE (EQ ←X ←Y))
                     (RETURN $X]

The GCD is the greatest common divisor.

6.6. Reasoning About Arrays

Most of the knowledge about arrays embedded in the system is expressed as simplification rules.

- (ACCESS (CHANGE A I T) I) = T,
  I $\neq$ J $\supset$ (ACCESS (CHANGE A I T) J) = (ACCESS A J):

      ACCH=(LAMBDA (ACCESS (CHANGE ←A ←I ←T)
                      ←J)
              (PROG (DECLARE)
                   (ATTEMPT (GOAL $DEDUCE (EQ $I $J))
                       THEN
                       (RETURN $T))
                 (GOAL $DEDUCE (NEQ $I $J))
                 (RETURN (ACCESS $A $J]

ACCH is one of the TOPRULES, as are the rules below, ACCEX, MAXONE, MAX, and MAXPLUS.

- (EXCHANGE A I J) is a higher-level function whose output is the array A with the values of A[I] and A[J] exchanged. The value of (ACCESS (EXCHANGE A I J) K) depends on whether or not K equals I or J, i.e., whether the element here accessed was affected by the exchange. If K = I, the value is A[J]. If K = J, the value is A[I]. If K is neither I nor J, the value is the original value of A[K], since the location has not been affected by the exchange. The rule fails if it cannot be determined whether or not K= I or K=J. This information is embodied in the rule ACCEX:

      ACCEX=(LAMBDA (ACCESS (EXCHANGE ←A ←I ←J)
                     ←K)
              (PROG (DECLARE)
                   (ATTEMPT (GOAL $DEDUCE (EQ $K $I))
                       THEN
                       (RETURN (ACCESS $A $J)))

```
                          (ATTEMPT (GOAL $DEDUCE (EQ $K $J))
                          THEN
                               (RETURN (ACCESS $A $I)))
                          (GOAL $DEDUCE (AND (NEQ $K $I)
                                             (NEQ $K $J)))
                          (RETURN (ACCESS $A $K]
```

• The maximum of an array, MAXA, is a function of three arguments: the array, the lower bound, and the upper bound.

$$(MAXA\ A\ I\ J) = (MAX\ A[I]\ ,\ A[I+1]\ ,\ ...,\ A[J]\ )$$

$$(MAXA\ A\ I\ I) = A[I]\ :$$

```
MAXONE=(LAMBDA (MAXA ←A ←I ←J)
               (PROG (DECLARE)
                     (GOAL $DEDUCE (EQ $I $J))
                     (RETURN (ACCESS $A $I]
```

• If

$$(MAXA\ A\ I\ J) \leqslant A[J+1]\ ,$$

then

$$(MAXA\ A\ I\ J+1) = A[J+1]\ .$$

On the other hand, if

$$(MAXA\ A\ I\ J)\ > A[J+1]\ ,$$

then

$$(MAXA\ A\ I\ J+1) = (MAXA\ A\ I\ J);$$

```
MAXPLUS=(LAMBDA
    (MAXA ←A ←I (PLUS ←J 1))
    (PROG (DECLARE)
          (ATTEMPT (GOAL $DEDUCE (LTQ (MAXA $A $I $J)
                                      (ACCESS $A (PLUS $J 1]
                   THEN
                   (RETURN (ACCESS $A (PLUS $J 1))))
          (GOAL $DEDUCE (LT (ACCESS $A (PLUS $J 1))
                            (MAXA $A $I $J))
          (RETURN (MAXA $A $I $J]
```

• Recall that (BAGA A I J) is (BAG A[I], A[I+1], ..., A[J]). Because of the crucial part this function plays in assertions about sortlike programs, we have many rules for it.

BAGARULES=
(TUPLE BAGAPLUS BAGAEMPTY BAGAII ARGSIMP BACH BAGEX BAGEX1
     BAGAMINUS BAGALOWERPLUS BAGEXCOMPLICATED)

- These rules are controlled by the rule BAGAOP, one of the TOPRULES:

    BAGAOP=(LAMBDA (PAND ←Y (BAGA ←←X))
                    ($TRYALLFAIL $BAGARULES $Y]

Thus, the BAGARULES will be tried whenever we are simplifying an expression of the form (BAGA A I J).

- If I ⩽ J+1, then (BAGA A I J+1) = (BAG A[J+1] (STRIP (BAGA A I J))):

    BAGAPLUS=(LAMBDA (BAGA ←A ←I (PLUS 1 ←J))
                    (PROG (DECLARE)
                    (GOAL $DEDUCE (LTQ $I (PLUS 1 $J)))
                    (RETURN (BAG (ACCESS $A (PLUS $J 1))
                            (STRIP (BAGA $A $I $J]

- If I < J, then (BAGA A J I) is the empty bag:

    BAGAEMPTY=(LAMBDA (BAGA ←A ←J ←I)
                    (PROG (DECLARE)
                    (GOAL $DEDUCE (LT $I $J))
                    (RETURN (BAG]

- (BAGA A I I) is (BAG A[I]):

    BAGAII=(LAMBDA (BAGA ←A ←I ←J)
                    (PROG (DECLARE)
                    (GOAL $DEDUCE (EQ $I $J))
                    (RETURN (BAG (ACCESS $A $I]

- If I ⩽ J, then (BAGA A I J) = (BAG (STRIP (BAGA A I J−1)) A[J]):

    BAGAMINUS=(LAMBDA (BAGA ←A ←I ←J)
                (PROG (DECLARE)
                    ($INSIST (EQUAL (STYPE $J)
                            IDENT))
                    (GOAL $DEDUCE (LTQ $I $J))
                    (RETURN (BAG (ACCESS $A $J)
                            (STRIP (BAGA $A $I (SUBTRACT $J 1]

Since this rule would apply so often, it is restricted by forcing J to be an identifier rather than a complex expression.

● If L ≤ M, then

　　(BAGA A L M) = (BAG A[L] (STRIP (BAGA A L+1 M))):

BAGALOWERPLUS=
(LAMBDA (BAGA ←ARNAME ←L ←M)
　　　(PROG (DECLARE F LOWER UPPER W)
　　　　　(EXISTS (←F ←←V (STRIP (BAGA $ARNAME ←LOWER
　　　　　　　　　　　　　　　　　　　　←UPPER))
　　　　　　　　　　　←←W))
　　　　　(GOAL $DEDUCE (EQ $LOWER (PLUS 1 $L)))
　　　　　(RETURN (BAG (ACCESS $ARNAME $L)
　　　　　　　　　　　(STRIP (BAGA $ARNAME (PLUS 1 $L)
　　　　　　　　　　　　$M]

This rule tries to determine if its application is desirable by checking in the
model for any relationship involving an array segment with lower bound equal
to L+1; if no such relationship exists, it is doubtful that the proposed simplification will lead to a proof.

● If I ≤ J ≤ K, then

　　　　　(BAGA (CHANGE A J T) I K) =

　　　　(BAG T (STRIP (BAGA A I K))) ~ (BAG A[J]).

On the other hand, if J < I or K < J,

　　　　　(BAGA (CHANGE A J T) I K) = (BAGA A I K).

(The notation ~ means the difference between two bags.) In other words,
making an assignment to an array element whose index is outside the bounds
of a segment does not affect the segment. However, if the index is within
bounds of the segment, then the corresponding bag will lose the old value of the
array element but gain the new value:

BACH=
(LAMBDA
　(BAGA (CHANGE ←A ←J ←T) ←I ←K)
　(PROG
　　(DECLARE)
　　(ATTEMPT
　　(GOAL $DEDUCE (LTQ $I $J $K))
　　THEN
　　(RETURN
　　　(=
　　　($TRY
　　　　$DIFFRULES

```
($TRYSUB
(TUPLE ACCH ACCEX)
ON
(' (ACCESS $A $J))
IN
($TRYSUB $BAGARULES ON ('(BAGA $A $I $K))
            IN
            (' (DIFFERENCE (BAG $T
                                (STRIP (BAGA $A $I $K)))
                           (BAG (ACCESS $A $J))))))))))))
(GOAL $DEDUCE (OR (LT $J $I)(LT $K $J)))
(RETURN (BAGA $A $I $K]
```

The rule BACH contains many recommendations about possible future simplifications. These recommendations are included to promote efficiency; the simplifier would eventually try the recommended rules even if the advice were omitted. The advice-giving functions TRY and TRYSUB are described in the section on utility functions.

• As mentioned above, (EXCHANGE A I J) is the array A with the values of A[I] and A[J] interchanged. If I and J are either both inside or both outside an array segment, then the exchange operation has no effect on the bag corresponding to that segment:

```
BAGEX = (LAMBDA (BAGA (EXCHANGE ←A ←I ←J) ←L ←M)
             (PROG (DECLARE)
             (GOAL $DEDUCE (LTQ $I $J))
             (ATTEMPT
             (GOAL $DEDUCE
                      (OR (AND (LTQ $L $I)
                               (LTQ $J $M)
                          (LT $J $L)
                          (LT $M $I)
                          (AND (LT $I $L)
                               (LT $M $J))))
             THEN
             (RETURN (BAGA $A $L $M) )
             ELSE
             (FAIL]
```

For simplicity, BAGEX requires that I ≤ J.

• If elements A[I] and A[J] are exchanged, and if J is in the array segment and I is not, or if I is in the segment and J is not, then the corresponding bag is indeed affected by the exchange operation. For instance, in the case in which J is in the segment and I is not, if the segment is bounded by L and M, the new bag is

$$(BAG\ (STRIP\ (BAGA\ A\ L\ J{-}1)$$
$$A[I]$$
$$(STRIP\ (BAGA\ A\ J{+}1M))):$$

BAGEX1=
(LAMBDA
 (BAGA (EXCHANGE ←A ←I ←J) ←L ←M)
 (PROG (DECLARE)
        (GOAL $DEDUCE (LTQ $I $J))
        (ATTEMPT (GOAL $DEDUCE (AND (LT $I $L)
                                    (LTQ $L $J)
                                    (LTQ $J $M)))
              THEN
              (RETURN (BAG (STRIP (BAGA $A $L (SUBTRACT $J 1)))
                           (ACCESS $A $I)
                           (STRIP (BAGA $A (PLUS 1 $J) $M))))
        (ATTEMPT (GOAL $DEDUCE (AND (LT $M $J)
                                    (LTQ $L $I)
                                    (LTQ $I $M)))
              THEN
              (RETURN (BAG (STRIP (BAGA $A $L (SUBTRACT $I 1)))
                           (ACCESS $A $J)
                           (STRIP (BAGA $A (PLUS 1 $I) $M))))
              ELSE
              (FAIL]

• BAGEXCOMPLICATED handles the case in which it can be determined that one of the exchanged elements is within or outside the array segment, but the location of the other array element is uncertain. The result is then a conditional expression. For example, if J is known to be outside the segment but I is only known to be greater than or equal to the lower limit L, the result is

$$(IF\ M < I\ THEN\ (BAGA\ A\ L\ M)$$
$$ELSE\ (BAG\ (STRIP\ (BAGA\ A\ L\ I{-}1))$$
$$A[J]$$
$$(STRIP\ (BAGA\ A\ I{+}1\ M))):$$

BAGEXCOMPLICATED=
(LAMBDA
 (BAGA (EXCHANGE ←A ←I ←J) ←L ←M)
 (PROG

```
(DECLARE)
(GOAL $DEDUCE (LTQ $I $J))
(ATTEMPT (GOAL $DEDUCE (AND (LTQ $L $I)
                            (LTQ $M $J)))
          THEN
          (RETURN (IFTHENELSE
                    (LT $M $I)
                    (BAGA $A $L $M)
                    (BAG (STRIP (BAGA $A $L (SUBTRACT $I 1)))
                    (ACCESS $A $J)
                    (STRIP (BAGA $A (PLUS 1 $I) $M))))))
(ATTEMPT (GOAL $DEDUCE (AND (LTQ $J $M)
                            (LTQ $L $J)))
          THEN
          (RETURN (IFTHENELSE
                    (LTQ $L $I)
                    (BAGA $A $L $M)
                    (BAG (STRIP (BAGA $A $L (SUBTRACT $J 1)))
                    (ACCESS $A $I)
                    (STRIP (BAGA $A (PLUS 1 $J) $M)))))
          ELSE
          (FAIL]
```

BAGEXCOMPLICATED comes after BAGEX and BAGEX1 in the goal class BAGARULES because we prefer the definite answer they provide to the conditional expression returned by BAGEXCOMPLICATED.

All the rules in this section have been simplification rules. There also are two inequalities rules that pertain to arrays, INEQSTRIPTRAN and INEQSTRIP-STRIP.

• To prove that every element in an array segment is less than (or less than or equal to) some quantity C, find an array segment that properly contains the given segment such that every element in the larger segment is less than some element D that is, in turn, less than or equal to C:

```
INEQSTRIPTRAN=
(LAMBDA (←F (STRIP (BAGA ←ARNAME ←L ←M))←C)
        (PROG (DECLARE LOWER UPPER D)
              (EXISTS ($F (STRIP (BAGA $ARNAME ←LOWER
                           ←UPPER)) ←D))
              (GOAL $DEDUCE (AND (LTQ $LOWER $L)
                                  (LTQ $M $UPPER)
                                  (LTQ $D $C]
```

• To prove some ordering relation < or ≤ between all the elements of two array segments, S_1 and S_2, find relations of the same sense involving $S_1{}'$ and C, and involving D and S_2'. Then show that S_1' and S_2' contain S_1 and S_2 respectively, and that C is less than or equal to D.

```
INEQSTRIPSTRIP=
(LAMBDA (←F (STRIP (BAGA ←A ←I ←J))
             (STRIP (BAGA ←A ←K ←L)))
         (PROG (DECLARE LOWER1 UPPER1 LOWER2 UPPER2 C D)
              (ATTEMPT (EXISTS ($F (STRIP (BAGA $A ←LOWER1
                                                ←UPPER1))
                               ←C))
                       (EXISTS ($F ←D
                                (STRIP (BAGA $A ←LOWER2
                                             ←UPPER2))))
                       (GOAL $DEDUCE (AND (LTQ $LOWER1 $I)
                                          (LTQ $J $UPPER1)
                                          (LTQ $LOWER2 $K)
                                          (LTQ $L $UPPER2)
                                          (LTQ $C $D)))
                       ELSE
                       (FAIL]
```

6.7. Reasoning About Bags

We have accumulated a number of rules about bags. Many of these rules have set-theoretic counterparts, which could have been included, but we have needed only bags in our proofs.

We use the QA4 function DIFFERENCE to mean the difference between bags, written informally as "∼".

- $(BAG\ x\ y) \sim (BAG\ x) = (BAG\ y)$:

```
DIFFXX=(LAMBDA (DIFFERENCE (BAG ←X ←←Y)
                           (BAG ←X))
               (BAG $$Y]
```

- $cons(x, y \sim z) = cons(x, y) \sim z$:

```
CONSDIFF=(LAMBDA (CONS ←X (DIFFERENCE ←Y ←←Z))
                 ( (DIFFERENCE (CONS $X $Y)
                              $$Z]
```

- $(x \sim y) \sim z = x \sim y \sim z$:

```
DIFDIF=(LAMBDA (DIFFERENCE (DIFFERENCE ←X ←←Y)
                           ←←Z)
               (' (DIFFERENCE $X $$Y $$Z]
```

- $cons(x, y) \sim (\text{BAG } x) \sim u = y \sim u$:

        DIFFCONS=(LAMBDA (DIFFERENCE (CONS ←X ←Y)
                                     (BAG ←X)
                                     ←←U)
                         ($TRY (TUPLE DIFFONE)
                               (' (DIFFERENCE $Y $$U]

- (DIFFERENCE x) is taken to be x itself:

        DIFFONE=(LAMBDA (DIFFERENCE ←X) $X)

- (BAG (STRIP x)) = x:

        BAGSTRIP=(LAMBDA (BAG (STRIP ←X)) $X)

6.8. Reasoning about Substitutions

The rules in this section were added to prove assertions about the pattern matcher and the unification algorithm.

- An atom is either a variable or a constant:

$$\neg var(x) \wedge \neg const(x) \supset \neg atom(x):$$

        NOTATOM=(LAMBDA (NOT (ATOM ←X))
                        (PROG (DECLARE)
                              (EXISTS (NOT (VAR $X)))
                              (EXISTS (NOT (CONST $X]

- If an expression is made of constants, so is the *car* and the *cdr* of the expression:

        CONSTCAR=(LAMBDA (CONSTEXP (CAR ←X))
                         (EXISTS (CONSTEXP $X]
        CONSTCDR=(LAMBDA (CONSTEXP (CDR ←X))
                         (EXISTS (CONSTEXP $X]

NOTATOM, CONSTCAR, and CONSTCDR are DEDUCE rules.

- The empty substitution does not change the expression:

        SUBSTEMPTY=(LAMBDA (VARSUBST EMPTY ←X) $X)

- No substitution changes an expression made up entirely of constants:

  SUBSTCONST=(LAMBDA (VARSUBST ←S ←Y)
          (PROG (DECLARE)
               (GOAL $DEDUCE (CONSTEXP $Y))
               $Y)

  SUBSTEMPTY and SUBSTCONST are simplification rules.

- To prove

$$varsubst(s, car(x)) = car(y),$$

prove

$$varsubst(s, x) = y:$$

  SUBSTCAR=(LAMBDA (EQ (VARSUBST ←S1 (CAR ←X))(CAR ←Y))
             (GOAL $EQRULES (EQ (VARSUBST $S1 $X)
                             $Y]

- Similarly, to prove

$$varsubst(s, cdr(x)) = cdr(y),$$

prove

$$varsubst(s, x) = y:$$

  SUBSTCDR=(LAMBDA (EQ (VARSUBST ←S1 (CDR ←X))(CDR ←Y))
             (GOAL $EQRULES (EQ (VARSUBST $S1 $X)
                             $Y]

- To prove

$$varsubst(s, x) = y,$$

where x and y are nonatomic, prove

$$varsubst(s, car(x)) = car(y)$$

and

$$varsubst(s, cdr(x)) = cdr(y):$$

  SUBSTCONS=
      (LAMBDA (EQ (VARSUBST ←S1 ←X) ←Y)
          (PROG (DECLARE)
              (GOAL $DEDUCE (NOT (ATOM $X)))
              (GOAL $DEDUCE (NOT (ATOM $Y)))

```
(GOAL (= ($REMOVE EQSUBST FROM $EQRULES))
       (EQ (VARSUBST $S1 (CAR $X))(CAR $Y)))
(GOAL (= ($REMOVE EQSUBST FROM $EQRULES))
       ( EQ (VARSUBST $S1 (CDR $X))(CDR $Y]
```

● SUBSTCAR, SUBSTCDR, and SUBSTCONS are equality rules. They are clustered together in a goal class:

```
EQSUBSTRULES=
(TUPLE SUBSTCAR SUBSTCDR SUBSTCARCDR SUBSTCONS)
```

● EQSUBSTRULES is called from EQSUBST, an EQRULE.

```
EQSUBST=(LAMBDA (PAND ←Y (EQ (VARSUBST ←S ←X) ←Z))
                (GOAL $EQSUBSTRULES $Y]
```

Note that SUBSTCONS removes EQSUBST from the EQRULES. This avoids the loop that would occur if SUBSTCAR were applied after SUBSTCONS.

● To prove
$$varsubst(s, u) = varsubst(s, v),$$
where u and v are nonatomic, prove
$$varsubst(s, car(u)) = varsubst(s, car(v))$$
and
$$varsubst(s, cdr(u)) = varsubst(s, cdr(v)):$$

```
SUBSTCARCDR=(LAMBDA (EQ (VARSUBST ←S ←U)
                        (VARSUBST ←S ←V))
                    (PROG (DECLARE)
                          (GOAL $DEDUCE (NOT (ATOM $U)))
                          (GOAL $DEDUCE (NOT (ATOM $V)))
                          (GOAL $EQRULES
                                (EQ (VARSUBST $S (CAR $U))
                                    (VARSUBST $S (CAR $V))))
                          (GOAL $EQRULES
                                (EQ (VARSUBST $S (CDR $U))
                                    (VARSBUST $S (CDR $V]
```

Substitutions are represented as lists of dotted pairs.

● If v is a variable,
$$varsubst(((v·y)), v) = y:$$

SUBSTLIST=(LAMBDA (VARSUBST (LIST (CONS ←V ←Y))←V)
                    (PROG (DECLARE)
                        (EXISTS (VAR $V)) $Y]

- The composition operator has the property

$$varsubst(compose(s1, s2), x) = varsubst(s1, varsubst(s2, x)):$$

SUBSTCOMPOSE=(LAMBDA (VARSUBST (COMPOSE ←S1 ←S2)←X)
                    ($TRY $SUBSTRULES
                            ('(VARSUBST $S1 (VARSUBST $S2 $X]

- These simplification rules are members of the goal class

SUBSTRULES=
        (TUPLE SUBSTEMPTY SUBSTLIST SUBSTCOMPOSE SUBSTCONST)

which is called by SUBSTOP, a member of TOPRULES:

SUBSTOP=(LAMBDA (PAND (VARSUBST ←←X)←Y)
                    (GOAL $SUBSTRULES $Y]

6.9. Utility Functions

- TRY is like a GOAL statement that will not fail if none of the goal class applies but instead returns its argument.

TRY=(LAMBDA (TUPLE ←GOALCLASS ←GOAL1)
                (ATTEMPT (GOAL $GOALCLASS $GOAL1)
                    ELSE $GOAL1]

It evaluates (GOAL $GOALCLASS $GOAL1), but, if failure results, it returns GOAL1.

- TRYALL will try a goal class on an expression. If any member of the goal class applies, it will apply the same goal class to the resulting expression, and so on, until no rule applies. TRYALL returns the last expression it has derived, which may be the same as the first expression; TRYALL will not fail:

TRYALL=
(LAMBDA (TUPLE ←GOALCLASS1 ←GOAL1)
        (PROG (DECLARE)
            TOP (ATTEMPT (SETQ ←GOAL1 (GOAL $GOALCLASS1
                                                    $GOAL1))
                            THEN
                            (GO TOP))
            (RETURN $GOAL1]

● TRYALLFAIL is like TRYALL, except it will fail if none of the goal class applies to the argument.

```
TRYALLFAIL=(LAMBDA (TUPLE ←GOALCLASS1 ←GOAL1)
                  ($TRYALL $GOALCLASS1
                          (GOAL $GOALCLASS1 $GOAL1]
```

● TRYSUB applies a goal class to a specially designated subexpression of the given expression:

```
TRYSUB=(LAMBDA (TUPLE ←GOALCLASS ON ←SUB IN ←EXP)
              (SUBST $EXP
                     (TUPLE $SUB ($TRYALL $GOALCLASS $SUB]
```

● INSIST fails if its argument is FALSE.

```
                  INSIST=(LAMBDA ←X (IF $X ELSE (FAIL]
```

● REMOVE removes a designated item from a tuple.

```
        REMOVE=(LAMBDA (TUPLE ←X FROM ←Y)
                      ((QUOTE (LAMBDA (TUPLE ←←U $X ←←V)
                                      (TUPLE $$U $$V)))
                      $Y]
```

● ASK queries the user:

```
                  ASK=(LAMBDA ←X
                              (IF (LISP ASK $X)
                              ELSE
                              (FAIL]
```

It types two expressions, the first a QA4 expression and the second an atom (e.g., PROVE? or SIMPLIFY?). If the user types YES, TRUE, OK, Y, or T, ASK returns TRUE; otherwise ASK fails. ASK uses a LISP function of the same name.

● SHORTEST computes the "smallest" element of a set, bag, or tuple:

```
SHORTEST=
(LAMBDA ←X
  (PROG (DECLARE BEST BESTCOUNT TEMPCOUNT)
        (SETQ ←BESTCOUNT 2000)
        (MAPC $X (QUOTE (LAMBDA ←Y
                        (IF (OR (LT (SETQ ←TEMPCOUNT
                                    (LISP QA4COUNT $Y))
```

TABLE 1.1
Index of Functions and Goal Classes

[a] Goal class.

$BESTCOUNT)
(EQUAL (STYPE $Y)
NUMBER))
THEN
(SETQ ←BEST $Y)
(SETQ ←BESTCOUNT $TEMPCOUNT)))))
$BEST]

The size of an expression is roughly the number of atoms in the expression. It is computed by a LISP function, QA4COUNT. Numbers are assumed to be "smaller" than identifiers.

Table 1.1 gives an index of functions and goal classes.

7. Appendix: Traces of Solutions

7.1. The Maximum of an Array (First Verification Condition)

A complete trace of a proof performed by our system is presented below. The verification condition to be proved is derived from the program to compute the maximal element of an array. Although a proof is contained above in the body of the text, following the trace tells us exactly what rules were applied in the proof. Furthermore, we can see exactly what false starts were made by the system and what user interaction was required to keep the program on the right track.

This particular verification condition was derived from the loop path of the program. The hypotheses are

```
 1  (CONTEXT (1 0) 1 0)
 2  (ASSERT (EQ MAX (ACCESS A LOC)) WRT $VERICON)
 3  TRUE
 4  (ASSERT (LTQ (STRIP (BAGA A 0 I)) MAX) WRT $VERICON)
 5  TRUE
 6  (ASSERT (LTQ 0 LOC) WRT $VERICON)
 7  TRUE
 8  (ASSERT (LTQ LOC I) WRT $VERICON)
 9  TRUE
10 (ASSERT (LTQ I N) WRT $VERICON)
11 TRUE
12 (DENY (LT N (PLUS 1 I)) WRT $VERICON)
13 FALSE
14 (DENY (LT MAX (ACCESS A (PLUS 1 I))) WRT $VERICON)
15 FALSE
```

Since the hypotheses for the different verification conditions of a program may contradict each other, each proof is done in a separate context. The name of that context is VERICON. That is the meaning of the phrase "WRT $VERI-CON" which follows our assertions and goal. [For this proof, VERICON is ((1 0) 1 0).] Assertions made with respect to one VERICON will not affect problems solved with respect to another.

16 (GOAL $PROVE (LTQ (STRIP (BAGA A 0 (PLUS 1 I))) MAX) WRT
                $VERICON)
17   LAMBDA PROOFSWITCH (LTQ (STRIP (BAGA A 0 (PLUS 1 I))) MAX)

When a traced function is applied to an argument, the trace says

                LAMBDA ⟨function name⟩ ⟨argument⟩.

Some of the utility functions are not traced.

18 (GOAL $INEQUALITIES ($F $X))
19   LAMBDA RELCHECK (LTQ (STRIP (BAGA A 0 (PLUS 1 I))) MAX)
20   LAMBDA PROOFSIMP (LTQ (STRIP (BAGA A 0 (PLUS 1 I))) MAX)
21   LAMBDA ARGSIMP (LTQ (STRIP (BAGA A 0 (PLUS 1 I))) MAX)
22   LAMBDA SIMPONE (TUPLE STRIP (BAGA A 0 (PLUS 1 I))) MAX)
  (TUPLE (STRIP (BAGA A 0 (PLUS 1 I))) MAX)
  SIMPLIFY?
  :Y

The system asked us whether we wanted it to simplify

        (TUPLE (STRIP (BAGA A 0 (PLUS 1 I))) MAX).

We said yes.

23   (GOAL $TOPRULES $GOAL1)
24   LAMBDA HASSIMP (TUPLE (STRIP (BAGA A 0 (PLUS 1 I))) MAX)
25   (FAIL)
26   LAMBDA EQNUMB (TUPLE (STRIP (BAGA A 0 (PLUS 1 I))) MAX)
27   (FAIL)
28   (GOAL $DOWNRULES $GOAL1)
29   LAMBDA TUPSIMP (TUPLE (STRIP (BAGA A 0 (PLUS 1 I))) MAX)
30   LAMBDA SIMPONE (STRIP (BAGA A 0 (PLUS 1 I)))
  (STRIP (BAGA A 0 (PLUS 1 I)))
  SIMPLIFY?
  :Y
31   (GOAL $TOPRULES $GOAL1)
32   LAMBDA HASSIMP (STRIP (BAGA A 0 (PLUS 1 I)))
33   (FAIL)
34   LAMBDA EQNUMB (STRIP (BAGA A 0 (PLUS 1 I)))

```
35        (FAIL)
36        (GOAL $DOWNRULES (GOAL1)
37         LAMBDA ARGSIMP (STRIP (BAGA A 0 (PLUS 1 I)))
38         LAMBDA SIMPONE (BAGA A 0 (PLUS 1 I))
   (BAGA A 0 (PLUS 1 I))
   SIMPLIFY?
   :Y
```

We have given the system permission to simplify (BAGA A 0 (PLUS 1 I)).

```
39        (GOAL $TOPRULES $GOAL1)
40         LAMBDA HASSIMP (BAGA A 0 (PLUS 1 I))
41        (FAIL)
42         LAMBDA BAGAOP (BAGA A 0 (PLUS 1 I))
43        (GOAL $GOALCLASS1 $GOAL1)
44         LAMBDA BAGAPLUS (BAGA A 0 (PLUS 1 I))
45        (GOAL $DEDUCE (LTQ $I (PLUS 1 $J)))
```

The system tries to prove that $0 \leqslant (\text{PLUS } 1 \text{ I})$.

```
46         LAMBDA RELCHECK (LTQ 0 (PLUS 1 I))
47         LAMBDA LTQPLUS (LTQ 0 (PLUS 1 I))
48        (GOAL $DEDUCE (AND (LTQ $I $J) (LTQ 0 $K)))
49         LAMBDA RELCHECK (AND (LTQ 0 I) (LTQ 0 1))
```

It breaks down the goal to $0 \leqslant I$ and $0 \leqslant 1$.

```
50         LAMBDA ANDSPLIT (AND (LTQ 0 I)(LTQ 0 1))
51        (GOAL $GOALCLASS $X)
52         LAMBDA RELCHECK (LTQ 0 1)
53         RELCHECK = TRUE
```

When a function returns a value, the trace says

$$\langle \text{function name} \rangle = \langle \text{value} \rangle.$$

In this case, the system knew that $0 < 1$ by performing the corresponding LISP evaluation.

```
54        (GOAL $GOALCLASS $Y)
55         LAMBDA RELCHECK (LTQ 0 I)
56         RELCHECK = TRUE
```

The $0 \leqslant I$ follows from the hypotheses 6 and 8.

```
57         ANDSPLIT = TRUE
58         LTQPLUS = TRUE
59         BAGAPLUS = (BAG (ACCESS A (PLUS 1 I)) (STRIP
           (BAGA A 0 I)))
```

The system has succeeded in simplifying

$$(BAGA\ A\ 0\ (PLUS\ 1\ I))$$

to

$$(BAG\ (ACCESS\ A\ (PLUS\ 1\ I))\ (STRIP\ (BAGA\ A\ 0\ I))).$$

```
60          (GOAL $GOALCLASS1 $GOAL1)
61           BAGAOP = (BAG (ACCESS A (PLUS 1 I)) (STRIP (BAGA
                    A 0 I)))
62           SIMPONE = (BAG (ACCESS A (PLUS 1 I)) (STRIP (BAGA
                    A 0 I)))
63           ARGSIMP = (STRIP (BAG (ACCESS A (PLUS 1 I)) (STRIP (BAGA
                    A 0 I))))
64          (GOAL $GOALCLASS $GOAL1)
65           LAMBA HASSIMP (STRIP (BAG (ACCESS A (PLUS 1 I))
                    (STRIP (BAGA A 0 I))))
66          (FAIL)
67           LAMBDA EQNUMB (STRIP (BAG (ACCESS A (PLUS 1 I)) (STRIP
                    (BAGA A 0 I))))
68          (FAIL)
69           SIMPONE = (STRIP (BAG (ACCESS A (PLUS 1 I)) (STRIP (BAGA
                    A 0 I))))
70           TUPSIMP = (TUPLE (STRIP (BAG (ACCESS A (PLUS 1 I)) (STRIP
                    (BAGA A 0 I)))) MAX)
71          (GOAL $GOALCLASS $GOAL1)
72           LAMBDA HASSIMP (TUPLE (STRIP (BAG (ACCESS A (PLUS 1 I))
                    (STRIP (BAGA A 0 I)))) MAX)
73          (FAIL)
74           LAMBDA EQNUMB (TUPLE (STRIP (BAG (ACCESS A (PLUS 1 I))
                    (STRIP (BAGA A 0 I)))) MAX)
75          (FAIL)
76           SIMPONE = (TUPLE (STRIP (BAG (ACCESS A (PLUS 1 I)) (STRIP
                    (BAGA A 0 I)))) MAX)
77           ARGSIMP = (LTQ (STRIP (BAG (ACCESS A (PLUS 1 I)) (STRIP (BAGA
                    A 0 I)))) MAX)
```

The problem now is to prove

$$(STRIP\ (BAG\ (ACCESS\ A\ (PLUS\ 1\ I))\ (STRIP\ (BAGA\ A\ 0\ I)))) \leqslant MAX:$$

```
78   (GOAL $GOALCLASS1 $X)
79    LAMBDA RELCHECK (LTQ (STRIP (BAG (ACCESS A (PLUS 1 I))
            (STRIP (BAGA A 0 I)))) MAX)
80    RELCHECK=TRUE
```

But since the system already knows

$$(ACCESS\ A\ (PLUS\ 1\ I)) \leqslant MAX \quad \text{from (14)},$$

and

$$(\text{STRIP (BAGA A 0 I)}) \leqslant \text{MAX} \quad \text{from (4),}$$

the proof is complete:

81   PROOFSIMP = TRUE
82   (ASSERT ($F $X))
83   PROOFSWITCH = (LTQ (STRIP (BAGA A 0 (PLUS 1 I))) MAX)
84   (LTQ (STRIP (BAGA A 0 (PLUS 1 I))) MAX)

7.2. The Maximum of an Array (Second Verification Condition)

The following is the trace of the proof for another verification condition for the program that computes the maximal element of an array. This verification condition is derived from the halt path of the program.

1   (CONTEXT (1 0) 1 0)
2   (ASSERT (EQ MAX (ACCESS A LOC)) WRT $VERICON)
3   TRUE
4   (ASSERT (LTQ (STRIP (BAGA A 0 I)) MAX) WRT $VERICON)
5   TRUE
6   (ASSERT (LTQ 0 LOC) WRT $VERICON)
7   TRUE
8   (ASSERT (LTQ LOC I) WRT $VERICON
9   TRUE
10 (ASSERT (LTQ I N) WRT $VERICON)
11 TRUE
12 (ASSERT (LT N (PLUS 1 I)) WRT $VERICON)

There is a demon that knows that in the integer domain,

$$x < y \supset x{+}1 \leqslant y.$$

This demon is responsible for the assertion

13 (ASSERT (LTQ (PLUS 1 $X) $Y) WRT $VERICON)

The system now knows $N{+}1 \leqslant I{+}1$. This assertion wakes up another demon, which asserts that $N \leqslant I$:

14 (ASSERT (LTQ $Y $Z) WRT $VERICON)
15 TRUE

Since $I \leqslant N$ has also been asserted (10), the mechanism for storing ordering relations silently tells the system that $I = N$.

The system proceeds with the proof:

16 (GOAL $PROVE (LTQ (STRIP (BAGA A 0 N)) (ACCESS A LOC)) WRT
    $VERICON)
17 LAMBDA PROOFSWITCH (LTQ (STRIP (BAGA A 0 N)) (ACCESS A
    LOC))
18 (GOAL $INEQUALITIES ($F $X))
19   LAMBDA RELCHECK (LTQ (STRIP) BAGA A 0 N)) (ACCESS A LOC))
20   LAMBDA PROOFSIMP (LTQ (STRIP (BAGA A 0 N)),(ACCESS A LOC))
21   LAMBDA ARGSIMP (LTQ (STRIP (BAGA A 0 N)) (ACCESS A LOC))
22   LAMBDA SIMPONE (TUPLE (STRIP (BAGA A 0 N)) (ACCESS A
    LOC))
  (TUPLE (STRIP (BAGA A 0 N)) (ACCESS A LOC))
  SIMPLIFY?
  :N
23   (FAIL)
24   (FAIL)
25   LAMBDA PROOFLEIB (LTQ (STRIP (BAGA A 0 N)) (ACCESS A LOC))
26   (EXISTS ($F ←Y))

The system searches the data base for an assertion of the form (LTQ ←Y),
i.e., the gross form of the goal we are trying to prove. It finds one [assertion
(4)] and asks us if it should try to prove that the argument of the assertion
it has found is equal to the argument of the goal:

  (EQ (TUPLE (STRIP (BAGA A 0 N)) (ACCESS A LOC)) (TUPLE (STRIP
    (BAGA A 0 I)) MAX))
  PROVE?

We say yes, the proof proceeds.

  :Y
27   (GOAL $EQRULES (EQ $X $Y))
28   LAMBDA RELCHECK (EQ (TUPLE (STRIP (BAGA A 0 N)) (ACCESS
    A LOC)) (TUPLE (STRIP (BAGA A 0 I)) MAX))
29   RELCHECK = TRUE
30   PROOFLEIB = TRUE
31 (ASSERT ($F $X))
32 PROOFSWITCH = (LTQ (STRIP (BAGA A 0 N)) (ACCESS A LOC))
33 (LTQ (STRIP (BAGA A 0 N)) (ACCESS A LOC))

The two tuples were found to be equal because N = I (from 10 and 14), and
MAX = A[LOC]. The proof is complete.

7.3. The Wensley Division Algorithm

The following is the complete trace of the proof included in the body of the
text:

1 (CONTEXT (1 0) 1 0)

2 (ASSERT (EQ AA (TIMES QQ YY)) WRT $VERICON)
3 TRUE
4 (ASSERT (EQ (TIMES 2 BB) (TIMES QQ DD)) WRT $VERICON)
5 TRUE
6 (ASSERT (LT PP (PLUS (TIMES QQ YY) (TIMES QQ DD))) WRT
        $VERICON)
7 TRUE
8 (ASSERT (LTQ (TIMES QQ YY) PP) WRT $VERICON)
9 TRUE
10 (ASSERT (LT PP (PLUS AA BB)) WRT $VERICON)
11 TRUE
12 (DENY (LT (DIVIDES DD 2) EE) WRT $VERICON)
13 FALSE

The goal is to prove $PP < QQ*YY + QQ*(DD/2)$:

14 (GOAL $PROVE (LT PP (PLUS (TIMES QQ YY) (TIMES QQ (DIVIDES
        DD 2)))) WRT $VERICON
15 LAMBDA PROOFSWITCH (LT PP (PLUS (TIMES QQ YY) (TIMES QQ
        (DIVIDES DD 2))))
16 (GOAL $INEQUALITIES ($F $X))
17 LAMBDA RELCHECK (LT PP (PLUS (TIMES QQ YY) (TIMES QQ
        (DIVIDES DD 2))))
18   LAMBDA PROOFSIMP (LT PP (PLUS (TIMES QQ YY) (TIMES QQ
        (DIVIDES DD 2))))
19   LAMBDA ARGSIMP (LT PP (PLUS (TIMES QQ YY) (TIMES QQ
        (DIVIDES DD 2))))
20   LAMBDA SIMPONE (TUPLE PP (PLUS (TIMES QQ YY) (TIMES
        QQ (DIVIDES DD 2))))
21   LAMBDA ASK (TUPLE PP (PLUS (TIMES QQ YY) (TIMES QQ
        (DIVIDES DD 2)))) SIMPLIFY?)
    (TUPLE PP (PLUS (TIMES QQ YY) (TIMES QQ (DIVIDES DD 2))))
    SIMPLIFY?
    :NO
22   (FAIL)
23   (FAIL)
24   LAMBDA PROOFLEIB (LT PP (PLUS (TIMES QQ YY) (TIMES QQ
        (DIVIDES DD 2))))
25   (EXISTS ($F ←Y))
26   LAMBDA ASK (TUPLE (EQ (TUPLE PP (PLUS (TIMES QQ YY)
                (TIMES QQ (DIVIDES DD 2))))
                (TUPLE PP (PLUS (TIMES QQ YY)
                (TIMES QQ DD)))) PROVE?)
    (EQ (TUPLE PP (PLUS (TIMES QQ YY) (TIMES QQ (DIVIDES DD 2))))
    (TUPLE PP (PLUS (TIMES QQ YY) (TIMES QQ DD))))
    PROVE?
    :NO

27   (FAIL)
28   LAMBDA ASK (TUPLE (EQ (TUPLE PP (PLUS (TIMES QQ YY)
               (TIMES QQ (DIVIDES DD 2))))
               (TUPLE PP (PLUS AA BB))) PROVE?)
    (EQ (TUPLE PP (PLUS (TIMES QQ YY) (TIMES QQ (DIVIDES DD 2))))
    (TUPLE PP (PLUS AA BB)))
    PROVE?
    :NO
29   (FAIL)
30   (LAMBDA INEQLEIB (LT PP (PLUS (TIMES QQ YY) (TIMES QQ
               (DIVIDES DD 2))))
31   (EXISTS ($L (TUPLE ←LOWER ←UPPER)))
32   LAMBDA ASK (TUPLE PROVE (LTQ PP PP) AND (LTQ (PLUS
               (TIMES QQ YY) (TIMES QQ DD))
               (PLUS (TIMES QQ YY) (TIMES
               QQ (DIVIDES DD 2))))?)
    PROVE
    (LTQ PP PP)
    AND
    (LTQ (PLUS (TIMES QQ YY) (TIMES QQ DD)) (PLUS (TIMES QQ YY)
    (TIMES QQ (DIVIDES DD 2))))
    ?
    :NO
33   (FAIL)

After several false starts, the system uses hypothesis (10), to generate two sub-goals: PP ⩽ PP and AA + BB ⩽ QQ*YY + QQ*(DD/2). We give our approval of this tactic:

34   LAMBDA ASK (TUPLE PROVE (LTQ PP PP) AND (LTQ (PLUS AA
               BB)(PLUS (TIMES QQ YY) (TIMES QQ (DIVIDES DD 2)))) ?)
    PROVE
    (LTQ PP PP)
    AND
    (LTQ (PLUS AA BB) (PLUS (TIMES QQ YY) (TIMES QQ (DIVIDES DD
    2))))
    ?
    :YES
35   ASK = TRUE

It proves the first subgoal immediately.

36   (GOAL $INEQUALITIES (AND (LTQ $X $LOWER) (LTQ $UPPER $Y)))
37   LAMBDA ANDSPLIT (AND (LTQ PP PP) (LTQ (PLUS AA BB) (PLUS
               TIMES QQ YY) (TIMES QQ (DIVIDES DD 2)))))
38   (GOAL $GOALCLASS $X)

```
39        LAMBDA RELCHECK (LTQ PP PP)
40        RELCHECK = TRUE
41        (GOAL $GOALCLASS (AND $$Y))
42          LAMBDA ANDSPLIT (AND (LTQ (PLUS AA BB)
                            (PLUS (TIMES QQ YY)
                            (TIMES QQ (DIVIDES DD 2)))))
43        (GOAL $GOALCLASS $X)
44          LAMBDA RELCHECK (LTQ (PLUS AA BB) (PLUS (TIMES
                            YY) (TIMES QQ (DIVIDES DD 2))))
45        LAMBDA INEQMONOTONE (LTQ (PLUS AA BB)(PLUS (TIMES
                            QQ YY) (TIMES QQ (DIVIDES DD 2))))
46          LAMBDA ASK (TUPLE ((LTQ AA (TIMES QQ (DIVIDES DD
                            2))) (LTQ BB (TIMES QQ YY))) PROVE?)
    ((LTQ AA (TIMES QQ DIVIDES DD 2))) (LTQ BB (TIMES QQ YY)))
    PROVE?
    :NO
47        (FAIL)
48        LAMBDA INEQMONOTONE (LTQ (PLUS AA BB) (PLUS (TIMES
                            QQ YY) (TIMES QQ (DIVIDES DD 2))))
49          LAMBDA ASK (TUPLE ((LTQ AA (TIMES QQ YY)) (LTQ BB
                            (TIMES QQ (DIVIDES DD 2)))) PROVE?)
    ((LTQ AA (TIMES QQ YY)) (LTQ BB (TIMES QQ (DIVIDES DD 2))))
    PROVE?
```

It divides the second subgoal into two sub-subgoals: $AA \leqslant QQ*YY$ and $BB \leqslant QQ*(DD/2)$:

```
    :YES
50        ASK = TRUE
51        (GOAL $GOALCLASS (AND ($F (TUPLE $W $Y)) ($F (TUPLE $X
                            $Z))))
52          LAMBDA ANDSPLIT (AND (LTQ AA (TIMES QQ YY)) (LTQ BB
                            (TIMES QQ (DIVIDES DD 2))))
53        (GOAL $GOALCLASS $X)
54          LAMBDA RELCHECK (LTQ AA (TIMES QQ YY))
55          RELCHECK = TRUE
```

The first sub-subgoal follows from hypothesis (2).

```
56        (GOAL $GOALCLASS (AND $$Y))
57          LAMBDA ANDSPLIT (AND LTQ BB (TIMES QQ (DIVIDES DD
                            2))))
58        (GOAL $GOALCLASS $X)
59          LAMBDA RELCHECK (LTQ BB (TIMES QQ (DIVIDES DD
                            2)))
```

```
60          LAMBDA INEQTIMESDIVIDE (LTQ BB (TIMES QQ (DIVIDES
                 DD 2)))
61          (GOAL $DEDUCE (LT 0 $Y))
62          LAMBDA RELCHECK (LT 0 2)
63          RELCHECK = TRUE
64          (GOAL $INEQUALITIES ($F (TUPLE (TIMES $Y $W) (TIMES
                 $X $$Z))))
65          LAMBDA RELCHECK (LTQ (TIMES 2 BB) (TIMES QQ DD))
66          RELCHECK = TRUE
```

Checking that $2 > 0$, the system multiplies out the second subgoal into $2*BB \leqslant QQ*DD$. This follows from assertion (4). The proof is complete:

```
67           INEQTIMESDIVIDE = TRUE
68           (GOAL $GOALCLASS (AND $$Y))
69           ANDSPLIT = (AND)
70           ANDSPLIT = (AND)
71          INEQMONOTONE = (AND)
72         (GOAL $GOALCLASS (AND $$Y))
73          ANDSPLIT = (AND)
74        ANDSPLIT = (AND)
75       INEQLEIB = (AND)
76     (ASSERT ($F $X))
77     (RETURN ($F $X))
78     PROOFSWITCH = (LT PP (PLUS (TIMES QQ YY) (TIMES QQ (DIVIDES
                 DD 2))))
79     (LT PP (PLUS (TIMES QQ YY) (TIMES QQ (DIVIDES DD 2))))
```

7.4. The Pattern Matcher

As an abbreviation, let

$$m1 = match(car(pat), car(arg))$$

and

$$m2 = match(varsubst(m1, cdr(pat)), cdr(arg)).$$

The hypotheses are that

$$varsubst(m1, car(pat)) = car(arg);$$

or, in unabbreviated form,

```
1   (ASSERT (EQ (VARSUBST (MATCH (CAR PAT) (CAR ARG))
    (CAR PAT)) (CAR ARG)))
2   TRUE
```

and that

$$varsubst(m2, varsubst(m1, cdr(pat))) = cdr(arg):$$

3 (ASSERT (EQ (VARSUBST (MATCH (VARSUBST (MATCH (CAR PAT)
 (CAR ARG)) (CDR PAT)) (CDR ARG)) (VARSUBST (MATCH (CAR PAT)
 (CAR ARG)) CDR PAT))) (CDR ARG)))
4 TRUE

The other hypotheses are

5 (ASSERT (CONSTEXP ARG))
6 TRUE
7 (ASSERT (NOT (CONST PAT)))
8 TRUE
9 (ASSERT (NOT (ATOM ARG)))
10 TRUE
11 (ASSERT (NOT (VAR PAT)))
12 TRUE

The goal is to prove

$$varsubst(compose(m2, m1), pat) = arg:$$

13 (GOAL $PROVE (EQ (VARSUBST (COMPOSE (MATCH (VARSUBST
 (MATCH (CAR PAT) (CAR ARG)) (CDR PAT)) (CDR ARG)) (MATCH
 (CAR PAT) (CAR ARG))) PAT) ARG))

The proof begins:

14 LAMBDA PROOFSWITCH (EQ (VARSUBST (COMPOSE (MATCH
 (VARSUBST (MATCH (CAR PAT) (CAR ARG)) (CDR PAT)) (CDR ARG))
 (MATCH (CAR PAT) (CAR ARG))) PAT) ARG)
15 (GOAL $EQRULES ($F $X))
16 LAMBDA RELCHECK (EQ (VARSUBST (COMPOSE (MATCH
 (VARSUBST (MATCH (CAR PAT) (CAR ARG)) (CDR PAT)) (CDR ARG))
 (MATCH (CAR PAT) (CAR ARG))) PAT) ARG)
17 LAMBDA EQSUBST (EQ (VARSUBST (COMPOSE (MATCH (VARSUBST
 (MATCH (CAR PAT) (CAR ARG)) (CDR PAT)) (CDR ARG)) (MATCH
 (CAR PAT) (CAR ARG))) PAT) ARG)
18 (GOAL $EQSUBSTRULES $Y)
19 LAMBDA SUBSTCONS (EQ (VARSUBST (COMPOSE (MATCH
 (VARSUBST (MATCH (CAR PAT) (CAR ARG)) (CDR PAT)) (CDR
 ARG)) (MATCH (CAR PAT) (CAR ARG))) PAT) ARG)
20 (GOAL $DEDUCE (NOT (ATOM $X)))
21 LAMBDA RELCHECK (NOT (ATOM PAT))

22   LAMBDA NOTATOM (NOT (ATOM PAT))
23   (EXISTS (NOT (VAR $X)))
24   (EXISTS (NOT (CONST $X)))
25   NOTATOM = (NOT (CONST PAT))
26   (GOAL $DEDUCE (NOT (ATOM $Y)))
27   (GOAL (= ($REMOVE (TUPLE EQSUBST FROM $EQRULES)))
        (EQ (VARSUBST $S1 (CAR $X)) (CAR $Y)))

Reasoning that *pat* is not an atom because it is neither a variable nor a constant, the system breaks the goal into two subgoals:

$$varsubst(compose(m2, m1), car(pat)) = car(arg)$$
and

$$varsubst(compose(m2, m1), cdr(pat)) = cdr(arg).$$

It begins work on the first of these:

28   LAMBDA RELCHECK (EQ (CAR ARG) (VARSUBST (COMPOSE
        (MATCH (VARSUBST (MATCH (CAR PAT) (CAR ARG))) (CDR
        PAT)) (CDR ARG)) (MATCH (CAR PAT) (CAR ARG))) (CAR PAT)))
29   LAMBDA EQSIMP (EQ (CAR ARG) (VARSUBST (COMPOSE
        (MATCH (VARSUBST (MATCH (CAR PAT) (CAR ARG))) (CDR PAT))
        (CDR ARG)) (MATCH (CAR PAT) (CAR ARG))) (CAR PAT)))
30   LAMBDA SIMPONE (VARSUBST (COMPOSE (MATCH (VARSUBST
        (MATCH (CAR PAT) (CAR ARG))) (CDR PAT)) (CDR ARG)) (MATCH
        (CAR PAT) (CAR ARG))) (CAR PAT))
     (VARSUBST (COMPOSE (MATCH (VARSUBST (MATCH (CAR PAT) (CAR
     ARG)) (CDR PAT)) (CDR ARG)) (MATCH (CAR PAT) (CAR ARG))) (CAR
     PAT))
     SIMPLIFY?

We give the system our permission to simplify the left side of the first subgoal,

$$varsubst(compose(m2, m1), car(pat)):$$

31   (GOAL $TOPRULES $GOAL1)
32   LAMBDA HASSIMP (VARSUBST (COMPOSE (MATCH (VARSUBST
        (MATCH (CAR PAT) (CAR ARG))) (CDR PAT)) (CDR ARG))
        (MATCH (CAR PAT) (CAR ARG))) (CAR PAT))
33   (FAIL)
34   LAMBDA SUBSTOP (VARSUBST (COMPOSE (MATCH
        (VARSUBST (MATCH (CAR PAT) (CAR ARG))) (CDR PAT))
        (CDR ARG)) (MATCH (CAR PAT) (CAR ARG))) (CAR PAT))
35   (GOAL $SUBSTRULES $Y)
36   LAMBDA SUBSTCOMPOSE (VARSUBST (COMPOSE (MATCH
          (VARSUBST (MATCH (CAR PAT) (CAR ARG))) (CDR PAT))
          (CDR ARG)) (MATCH (CAR PAT) (CAR ARG))) (CAR PAT))

37   (GOAL $GOALCLASS $GOAL1)
38   LAMBDA SUBSTCONST (VARSUBST (MATCH (VARSUBST
            (MATCH (CAR PAT) (CAR ARG)) (CDR PAT)) (CDR ARG))
            (VARSUBST (MATCH (CAR PAT) (CAR ARG)) (CAR PAT)))
39   (GOAL $DEDUCE (CONSTEXP $Y))
40   LAMBDA RELCHECK (CONSTEXP (VARSUBST (MATCH
            (CAR PAT) (CAR ARG)) (CAR PAT)))
41   SUBSTCOMPOSE = (VARSUBST (MATCH (VARSUBST (MATCH
            (CAR PAT) (CAR ARG)) (CDR PAT)) (CDR ARG)) (VARSUBST
            (MATCH (CAR PAT) (CAR ARG)) (CAR PAT)))
42   SUBSTOP = (VARSUBST (MATCH (VARSUBST (MATCH (CAR
            PAT) (CAR ARG)) (CDR PAT)) (CDR ARG)) (VARSUBST (MATCH
            (CAR PAT) (CAR ARG)) (CAR PAT)))
43   (RETURN $SIMPGOAL)
44   SIMPONE = (VARSUBST (MATCH (VARSUBST (MATCH (CAR PAT)
            (CAR ARG)) (CDR PAT)) (CDR ARG)) (VARSUBST (MATCH (CAR
            PAT) (CAR ARG)) (CAR PAT)))

The system has succeeded in simplifying the left half of the goal into

$$varsubst(m2, varsubst(m1, car(pat))).$$

It now tries to prove this new expression equal to *car(arg)*. In sympathy with
our conscientious readers, we omit portions of the remainder of the trace.

55   LAMBDA SIMPONE (VARSUBST (MATCH (VARSUBST (MATCH
            (CAR PAT) (CAR ARG)) (CDR PAT)) (CDR ARG)) (VARSUBST
            (MATCH (CAR PAT) (CAR ARG)) (CAR PAT)))
            (VARSUBST (MATCH (VARSUBST (MATCH (CAR PAT) (CAR ARG))
            (CDR PAT)) (CDR ARG)) (VARSUBST (MATCH (CAR PAT) (CAR ARG))
            (CAR PAT)))
            SIMPLIFY?

The system asks permission to simplify

$$varsubst(m1, varsubst(m2, car(pat)))$$

further. Permission is granted. We omit a portion of the trace.

The system wants to simplify *varsubst(m1, car(pat))*, a subexpression of our
goal. We give our blessings:

:Y
80   (GOAL $TOPRULES $GOAL1)
81   LAMBDA HASSIMP·(VARSUBST (MATCH (CAR PAT)
            (CAR ARG)) (CAR PAT))
82   (FAIL)

83   LAMBDA SUBSTOP (VARSUBST (MATCH (CAR PAT)
                           (CAR ARG)) (CAR PAT))
84   (GOAL $SUBSTRULES $Y)
85   LAMBDA SUBSTCONST (VARSUBST (MATCH (CAR
                           PAT) (CAR ARG)) (CAR PAT))
86   (GOAL $DEDUCE (CONSTEXP $Y))
87   LAMBDA RELCHECK (CONSTEXP (CAR PAT))
88   LAMBDA CONSTCAR (CONSTEXP (CAR PAT))
89   (EXISTS (CONSTEXP $X))
90   LAMBDA EQNUMB (VARSUBST (MATCH (CAR
                           PAT) (CAR ARG)) (CAR PAT))
91   (RETURN $BEST)
92   EQNUMB = (CAR ARG)
93   (RETURN $SIMPGOAL)
94   SIMPONE = (CAR ARG)

The subexpression *varsubst(m1, car(pat))* is known to be equal to *car(arg)* by
hypothesis (1). The rule EQNUMB has found this simplification. Work continues
on simplifying the entire left-hand side.

95   TUPSIMP = (TUPLE (MATCH (VARSUBST (MATCH
                           (CAR PAT) (CAR ARG)) (CDR PAT)) (CDR ARG))
                           (CAR ARG))
96   GOAL $GOALCLASS $GOAL1)
97   LAMBDA HASSIMP (TUPLE (MATCH (VARSUBST
                           (MATCH (CAR PAT) (CAR ARG)) (CDR PAT)) (CDR
                           ARG)) (CAR ARG))
98   (FAIL)
99   LAMBDA EQNUMB (TUPLE (MATCH (VARSUBST
                           (MATCH (CAR PAT) (CAR ARG)) (CDR PAT)) (CDR
                           ARG)) (CAR ARG))
100   (FAIL)
101   (RETURN $SIMPGOAL)
102   SIMPONE = (TUPLE (MATCH (VARSUBST (MATCH
                           (CAR PAT) (CAR ARG)) (CDR PAT)) (CDR ARG))
                           (CAR ARG))
103   ARGSIMP = (VARSUBST (MATCH (VARSUBST (MATCH
                           (CAR PAT) (CAR ARG)) (CDR PAT)) (CDR ARG)) (CAR
                           ARG))

The expression being simplified is now *varsubst(m2, car(arg))*:

104   (GOAL $GOALCLASS $GOAL1)
105   LAMBDA HASSIMP (VARSUBST (MATCH (VARSUBST
                           (MATCH (CAR PAT) (CAR ARG)) (CDR PAT)) (CDR
                           ARG)) (CAR ARG))

106	(FAIL)
107	LAMBDA SUBSTOP (VARSUBST (MATCH (VARSUBST (MATCH (CAR PAT) (CAR ARG)) (CDR PAT)) (CDR ARG)) (CAR ARG))
108	(GOAL $SUBSTRULES $Y)
109	LAMBDA SUBSTCONST (VARSUBST (MATCH (VARSUBST (MATCH (CAR PAT) (CAR ARG)) (CDR PAT)) (CDR ARG)) (CAR ARG))
110	(GOAL $DEDUCE (CONSTEXP $Y))
111	LAMBDA RELCHECK (CONSTEXP (CAR ARG))
112	LAMBDA CONSTCAR (CONSTEXP (CAR ARG))
113	(EXISTS (CONSTEXP $X))
114	CONSTCAR = (CONSTEXP ARG)
115	SUBSTCONST = (CAR ARG)
116	SUBSTOP = (CAR ARG)
117	(RETURN $SIMPGOAL)
118	SIMPONE = (CAR ARG)

Since *arg* consists entirely of constants, so does *car(arg)*. Therefore, substitutions have no effect on *car(arg)*, and the left-hand side of our subgoal reduces to *car(arg)* itself, which is precisely the same as the right-hand side.

119	(GOAL $EQRULES (EQ $X $Y))
120	LAMBDA RELCHECK (EQ (CAR ARG))
121	RELCHECK = TRUE
122	EQSIMP = TRUE
123	EQSIMP = TRUE

We omit the trace for the proof of the second subgoal,

$$varsubst(compose(m2, m1), cdr(pat)) = cdr(arg).$$

This subgoal is simplified to

$$varsubst(m2, varsubst(m1, cdr(pat))) = cdr(arg),$$

which is precisely our hypothesis (line 3).

142	(GOAL $EQRULES (EQ $X $Y))
143	EQSIMP = (EQ (VARSUBST (MATCH (VARSUBST (MATCH (CAR PAT) (CAR ARG)) (CDR PAT)) (CDR ARG)) (VARSUBST (MATCH (CAR PAT) (CAR ARG)) (CDR PAT))) (CDR ARG))
144	SUBSTCONS = (EQ (VARSUBST (MATCH (VARSUBST (MATCH (CAR PAT) (CAR ARG)) (CDR PAT)) (CDR ARG)) (VARSUBST (MATCH (CAR PAT) (CAR ARG)) (CDR PAT))) (CDR ARG))
145	EQSUBST = (EQ (VARSUBST (MATCH (VARSUBST (MATCH (CAR PAT) (CAR ARG)) (CDR PAT)) (CDR ARG)) (VARSUBST (MATCH (CAR PAT) (CAR ARG)) (CDR PAT))) (CDR ARG))

146   (ASSERT ($F $X))
147   (RETURN ($F $X))
148 PROOFSWITCH = (EQ (VARSUBST (COMPOSE (MATCH (VARSUBST
       (MATCH (CAR PAT) (CAR ARG)) (CDR PAT)) (CDR ARG)) (MATCH
       (CAR PAT) (CAR ARG))) PAT) ARG)
149 (EQ (VARSUBST (COMPOSE (MATCH (VARSUBST (MATCH (CAR PAT)
       (CAR ARG)) (CDR PAT)) (CDR ARG)) (MATCH (CAR PAT)
       (CAR ARG))) PAT) ARG)

The proof is complete.

7.5. The FIND Program

Only a selection from the trace for the interesting verification condition of
FIND is presented here because the entire trace was more than 500 lines long.
We will focus on the use of the case analysis during the proof.

The antecedent hypotheses for this condition are

$$1 \leqslant M \leqslant F \leqslant NN$$

$$M \leqslant I$$

$$J \leqslant N$$

$$(STRIP (BAGA A I M-1)) \leqslant (STRIP (BAGA A M NN))$$

$$(STRIP (BAGA A I N)) \leqslant (STRIP (BAGA A N+1 NN))$$

$$(STRIP (BAGA A 1 I-1)) \leqslant R$$

$$R \leqslant (STRIP (BAGA A 1+J NN))$$

$$A[J] \leqslant R$$

$$R \leqslant A[I]$$

$$I \leqslant J$$

$$J-1 < I+1$$

$$F \leqslant J-1$$

The theorem to be proved is

$$(STRIP (BAGA (EXCHANGE A I J) 1 J-1))$$

$$\leqslant (STRIP (BAGA (EXCHANGE A I J) (J-1)+1 NN)).$$

This goal is simplified to

$$(IF J-1 < I THEN (STRIP (BAGA A 1 J-1))$$

$$ELSE (STRIP (BAG (STRIP (BAGA A 1 I-1))$$

A[J]

(STRIP (BAGA A I+1 J−1)))))

≤ (IF J ≤ I THEN (STPIP) (BAGA A J NN)

ELSE (STRIP (BAG A[I]

(STRIP (BAGA A J+1 NN))

(STRIP (BAGA A J J−1))))):

1 (GOAL $INEQUALITIES (LTQ (IFTHENELSE (LT (SUBTRACT J 1) I)
(STRIP (BAGA A 1 (SUBTRACT J 1))) (STRIP (BAG (STRIP (BAGA A 1
(SUBTRACT I 1))) (ACCESS A J) (STRIP (BAGA A (PLUS 1 I) (SUBTRACT
J 1)))))) (IFTHENELSE (LTQ J I) (STRIP (BAGA A J NN)) (STRIP (BAG
(ACCESS A I) (STRIP (BAGA A (PLUS 1 J) NN)) (STRIP (BAGA A J
(SUBTRACT J 1))))))))

2 LAMBDA RELCHECK (LTQ (IFTHENELSE (LT (SUBTRACT J 1) I)
(STRIP (BAGA A 1 (SUBTRACT J 1))) (STRIP (BAG (STRIP (BAGA A 1
(SUBTRACT I 1))) (ACCESS A J) (STRIP (BAGA A (PLUS 1 I)
(SUBTRACT J 1)))))) (IFTHENELSE (LTQ J I) (STRIP (BAGA A J NN)
(STRIP (BAG (ACCESS A I) (STRIP (BAGA A (PLUS 1 J) NN)) (STRIP
(BAGA A J (SUBTRACT J 1))))))

3 LAMBDA INEQIFTHENELSE (LTQ (IFTHENELSE (LT (SUBTRACT J 1)
I) (STRIP (BAGA A 1 (SUBTRACT J 1))) (STRIP (BAG (STRIP (BAGA
A 1 (SUBTRACT I 1))) (ACCESS A J) (STRIP (BAGA A (PLUS 1 I)
(SUBTRACT J 1)))))) (IFTHENELSE (LTQ J I) (STRIP (BAGA A J NN))
(STRIP (BAG (ACCESS A I) (STRIP (BAGA A (PLUS 1 J) NN)) (STRIP
(BAGA A J (SUBTRACT J 1)))))))

4 (ASSERT $X WRT $VERICON)

Since the left side of the goal has an IF-THEN-ELSE form, it causes the rule
INEQIFTHENELSE to be applied. This rule sets VERICON to be a new lower
context and asserts

J−1 < I

with respect to the new VERICON. This question triggers off a demon:

5 (ASSERT (LTQ (PLUS 1 $X) $Y) WRT $VERICON)

The new assertion is

(J−1)+1 ≤ I.

The new assertion triggers off another demon, which makes still another assertion with respect to VERICON:

6 (ASSERT (LTQ $W $Y) WRT $VERICON)

This new assertion is

$$J \leqslant I.$$

(Later in the proof, another context will be established; $J-1 < I$ will be *denied* with respect to the new context.)

The THEN clause of the IF-THEN-ELSE expression must now be proved less than or equal to the right side of the goal:

7   (GOAL $INEQUALITIES ($F (TUPLE $$W1 $Y $$W2)) WRT $VERICON)

This goal is attempted with respect to the new context VERICON. In other words, we are trying to prove

(STRIP (BAGA A 1 J−1))

$\leqslant$ (IF J $\leqslant$ I THEN (STRIP (BAGA A J NN))

       ELSE (STRIP (BAG A[I]

              (STRIP (BAGA A J+1 NN))

              (STRIP (BAGA A J J−1)))))

with respect to the context in which $J \leqslant I$ has been asserted:

8   LAMBDA RELCHECK (LTQ (STRIP (BAGA A 1 (SUBTRACT J 1)))
    (IFTHENELSE (LTQ J I) (STRIP (BAGA A J NN)) (STRIP (BAG
    (ACCESS A I) (STRIP (BAGA A (PLUS 1 J) NN)) (STRIP (BAGA
    A J (SUBTRACT J 1)))))))
9   LAMBDA INEQIFTHENELSE (LTQ (STRIP (BAGA A 1 (SUBTRACT J
    1))) (IFTHENELSE (LTQ J 1) (STRIP (BAGA A J NN)) (STRIP (BAG
    (ACCESS A I) (STRIP (BAGA A (PLUS 1 J) NN)) (STRIP (BAGA A J
    (SUBTRACT J 1)))))))

Since the right side of the inequality is still in IF-THEN-ELSE form, the rule INEQIFTHENELSE applies again. A new context VERICON, even lower than the last, is established, and the (redundant) statement

$$J \leqslant I$$

is asserted with respect to the new context:

10   (ASSERT $X WRT $VERICON)

A new goal is established with respect to the new context.

11   (GOAL $INEQUALITIES ($F (TUPLE $$W1 $Y $$W2)) WRT $VERICON)

The new goal is

$$(STRIP (BAGA A 1 J-1)) \leqslant (STRIP (BAGA A J NN))$$

12	LAMBDA RELCHECK (LTQ (STRIP (BAGA A 1 (SUBTRACT J 1))) (STRIP (BAGA A J NN)))
13	LAMBDA PROOFSIMP (LTQ (STRIP (BAGA A 1 (SUBTRACT J 1))) (STRIP (BAGA A J NN)))
14	LAMBDA ARGSIMP (LTQ (STRIP (BAGA A 1 (SUBTRACT J 1))) (STRIP (BAGA A J NN)))
15	LAMBDA SIMPONE (TUPLE (STRIP (BAGA A 1 (SUBTRACT J 1))) (STRIP (BAGA A J NN)))

The simplifier is invoked. We will omit some steps from the trace here and mention only that the rule BAGALOWERPLUS played an important part in the simplification of the second element of the tuple.

90	SIMPONE = (TUPLE (STRIP (BAGA A 1 (SUBTRACT J 1))) (STRIP (BAG (STRIP (BAGA A (PLUS 1 J)) NN)) (ACCESS A J))))
91	ARGSIMP = (LTQ (STRIP (BAGA A 1 (SUBTRACT J 1))) (STRIP (BAG (STRIP (BAGA A (PLUS 1 J)) NN)) (ACCESS A J))))
92	(GOAL $GOALCLASS1 $X)

The simplified goal is

$$(STRIP (BAGA A 1 J-1))$$

$$\leqslant (STRIP (BAG (STRIP (BAGA A J+1 NN)) A[J])):$$

| 93 | LAMBDA RELCHECK (LTQ (STRIP (BAGA A 1 (SUBTRACT J 1))) (STRIP (BAG (STRIP (BAGA A (PLUS 1 J)) NN)) (ACCESS A J)))) |
| 94 | LAMBDA INEQSTRIPBAG (LTQ (STRIP (BAGA A 1 (SUBTRACT J 1))) (STRIP (BAG (STRIP (BAGA A (PLUS 1 J)) NN)) (ACCESS A J)))) |

INEQSTRIPBAG breaks up the goal into two subgoals. The first of these goals is

$$(STRIP (BAGA A 1 J-1)) \leqslant (STRIP (BAGA A J+1 NN)):$$

| 95 | (GOAL $INEQUALITIES ($F (TUPLE $$W $X $$Z))) |
| 96 | LAMBDA RELCHECK (LTQ (STRIP (BAGA A 1 (SUBTRACT J 1))) (STRIP (BAGA A (PLUS 1 J) NN))) |

The rule INEQSTRIPSTRIP is applicable to this goal:

| 103 | LAMBDA INEQSTRIPSTRIP (LTQ (STRIP (BAGA A 1 (SUBTRACT J 1))) (STRIP (BAGA A (PLUS 1 J) NN))) |

Since it is known that

$$(STRIP (BAGA A 1 I-1)) \leqslant (STRIP (BAGA A J+1 NN)),$$

and, in this context, $J \leqslant I$, INEQSTRIPSTRIP succeeds. The other subgoal to be proved is

$$(STRIP (BAGA A 1 J-1)) \leqslant (STRIP (BAG A[J])):$$

143   (GOAL $INEQUALITIES ($F (TUPLE $$W (STRIP (BAG $$Y))
             $$Z)))
144   LAMBDA RELCHECK (LTQ (STRIP (BAGA A 1 (SUBTRACT
             J 1))) (STRIP (BAG (ACCESS A J))))

INEQSTRIPBAG applies again, splitting this goal into two subgoals, one of which is trivial.

145   LAMBDA INEQSTRIPBAG (LTQ (STRIP (BAGA A 1
             (SUBTRACT J 1))) (STRIP (BAG (ACCESS A J))))
146   (GOAL $INEQUALITIES ($F (TUPLE $$W $X $$Z)))

The nontrivial goal is

$$(STRIP (BAGA A 1 J-1)) \leqslant A[J]:$$

147   LAMBDA RELCHECK (LTQ (STRIP (BAGA A 1
             (SUBTRACT J 1))) (ACCESS A J))

This goal invokes the rule INEQSTRIPTRAN. We will examine the operation of this rule in detail:

154   LAMBDA INEQSTRIPTRAN (LTQ (STRIP (BAGA A 1
             (SUBTRACT J 1))) (ACCESS A J))
155   (EXISTS ($F (TUPLE (STRIP (BAGA $ARNAME ←LOWER
             ←UPPER)) ←D)))

The rule finds the hypothesis

$$(STRIP (BAGA A 1 I-1)) \leqslant R.$$

It tests if this relation is appropriate:

156   (GOAL $DEDUCE (AND (LTQ $LOWER $L) (LTQ $M
             $UPPER) (LTQ $D $C)))
157   LAMBDA RELCHECK (AND (LTQ 1 1) (LTQ (SUBTRACT
             J 1) (SUBTRACT I 1)) (LTQ R (ACCESS A J)))

The system is testing whether the array segment between 1 and I−1 includes the segment between 1 and J−1, and also whether R ≤ A[J] :

158	LAMBDA ANDSPLIT (AND (LTQ 1 1) (LTQ (SUBTRACT J 1) (SUBTRACT I 1)) (LTQ R (ACCESS A J)))
159	(GOAL $GOALCLASS $X)
160	LAMBDA RELCHECK (LTQ 1 1)
161	RELCHECK = TRUE
162	(GOAL $GOALCLASS (AND $$Y))
163	LAMBDA RELCHECK (AND (LTQ (SUBTRACT J 1) (SUBTRACT I 1)) (LTQ R (ACCESS A J)))
164	LAMBDA ANDSPLIT (AND (LTQ (SUBTRACT J 1) (SUBTRACT I 1)) (LTQ R (ACCESS A J)))
165	(GOAL $GOALCLASS $X)
166	LAMBDA RELCHECK (LTQ (SUBTRACT J 1) (SUBTRACT I 1))
167	RELCHECK = TRUE
168	(GOAL $GOALCLASS (AND $$Y))
169	LAMBDA RELCHECK (AND (LTQ R (ACCESS A J)))
170	LAMBDA ANDSPLIT (AND (LTQ R (ACCESS A J)))
171	(GOAL $GOALCLASS $X)
172	LAMBDA RELCHECK (LTQ R (ACCESS A J))
173	RELCHECK = TRUE
174	(GOAL $GOALCLASS (AND $$Y))
175	ANDSPLIT = (AND)
176	ANDSPLIT = (AND)
177	ANDSPLIT = (AND)

The tests prove to be successful, and INEQSTRIPTRAN returns

178	INEQSTRIPTRAN = (AND)

The trivial subgoal is achieved:

179	(GOAL $INEQUALITIES ($F (TUPLE $$W (STRIP (BAG $$Y)) $$Z)))
180	LAMBDA RELCHECK (LTQ (STRIP (BAGA A 1 (SUBTRACT J 1))) (STRIP (BAG)))
181	RELCHECK = TRUE

The call to INEQSTRIPBAG from line 145 returns successfully:

182	INEQSTRIPBAG = TRUE

The call to INEQSTRIPBAG from line 94 also returns:

183	INEQSTRIPBAG = TRUE

Thus, the goal established in line 11 has been successfully proved:

184   PROOFSIMP = TRUE

That goal was established by the rule INEQIFTHENELSE. This rule asserted $J \leqslant I$ with respect to a lower context and set up the goal with respect to that context. The rule now attempts to deny $J \leqslant I$ with respect to another context and to establish a new goal with respect to the new context.

185   (DENY $X WRT $VERICON)

However, $J \leqslant I$ was also asserted with respect to a higher context in line 6. Therefore, denying $J \leqslant I$ contradicts this assertion, causing the denial to fail. Since the situation is contradictory and could not arise, it is unnecessary to achieve the goal, and the call to INEQIFTHENELSE from line 9 returns successfully:

186   (RETURN (SUCCESS (TUPLE WITH INEQIFTHENELSE)))
187   INEQIFTHENELSE = (SUCCESS (TUPLE WITH INEQIFTHENELSE))

The goal established in line 7 has been achieved. This goal was set up by an earlier call to INEQIFTHENELSE (line 3) with respect to a context in which $J-1 < I$ was asserted (line 4). It is now necessary to set up a new goal with respect to a new context; in this new context, $J-1 < I$ is denied:

188   (DENY $X WRT $VERICON)

This denial activates a demon that denies

$$J \leqslant I:$$

189   LAMBDA TRYALL (TUPLE (TUPLE PLUSEMPTY PLUSSINGLE
          PLUSZERO PLUSPLUS PLUSMINUS PLUSDIFFERENCE
          PLUSCOMBINE PLUSNUMBER) (PLUS 1 I (MINUS 1)))
190   (GOAL $GOALCLASS1 $GOAL1)
191   LAMBDA PLUSMINUS (PLUS 1 I (MINUS 1))
192   PLUSMINUS = (PLUS 1)
193   (GOAL $GOALCLASS1 $GOAL1)
194   LAMBDA PLUSSINGLE (PLUS I)
195   PLUSSINGLE = I
196   (GOAL $GOALCLASS1 $GOAL1)
197   (RETURN $GOAL1)
198   TRYALL = I
199 (DENY (LTQ $W $RTSIDE) WRT $VERICON)

The new goal

$$(STRIP \ (BAG \ (STRIP \ (BAGA \ A \ 1 \ I-1)$$
$$A[J]$$
$$(STRIP \ (BAGA \ A \ I+1 \ J-1))))$$
$$\leqslant (IF \ J \leqslant I \ THEN \ (STRIP \ (BAGA \ A \ J \ NN))$$
$$ELSE \ (STRIP \ (BAG \ A[I]$$
$$(STRIP \ (BAGA \ A \ J+1 \ NN))$$
$$(STRIP \ (BAGA \ A \ J \ J-1))))$$

is established with respect to the new context:

200 (GOAL $INEQUALITIES ($F (TUPLE $$W1 $Z $$W2)) WRT $VERICON)
201   LAMBDA RELCHECK (LTQ (STRIP (BAG (STRIP (BAGA A 1
      (SUBTRACT I 1))) (ACCESS A J) (STRIP (BAGA A (PLUS 1 I)
      (SUBTRACT J 1))))) (IFTHENELSE (LTQ J I) (STRIP (BAGA A J NN))
      (STRIP (BAG (ACCESS A I) (STRIP (BAGA A (PLUS 1 J) NN)) (STRIP
      (BAGA A J (SUBTRACT J 1)))))))

INEQIFTHENELSE is invoked because the right-side of the goal is of the form
IF-THEN-ELSE.

202   LAMBDA INEQIFTHENELSE (LTQ (STRIP (BAG (STRIP (BAGA A 1
      (SUBTRACT I 1))) (ACCESS A J) (STRIP (BAGA A (PLUS 1 I)
      (SUBTRACT J 1))))) (IFTHENELSE (LTQ J I) (STRIP (BAGA A J NN))
      (STRIP (BAG (ACCESS A I) (STRIP (BAGA A (PLUS 1 J) NN)) (STRIP
      (BAGA A J (SUBTRACT J 1)))))))

Again the rule creates two contexts: In one context $J \leqslant I$ is asserted, and in the
other $J \leqslant I$ is denied. However, since $J \leqslant I$ was denied in a higher context (line
199), the assertion of $J \leqslant I$ fails; this contradictory case can safely be ignored,
and attention focuses on the second context:

204   (DENY $X WRT $VERICON)

The goal is established using the ELSE clause of the previous goal,

$$(STRIP \ (BAG \ (STRIP \ (BAGA \ A \ 1 \ I-1))$$
$$A[J]$$
$$(STRIP \ (BAGA \ A \ I+1 \ J-1))))$$
$$\leqslant (STRIP \ (BAG \ A[I]$$

$$(STRIP \ (BAGA \ A \ J+1 \ NN))$$

$$(STRIP \ (BAGA \ A \ J \ J-1))))):$$

205 (GOAL $INEQUALITIES ($F (TUPLE $$W1 $Z $$W2)) WRT
$VERICON)

206 LAMBDA RELCHECK (LTQ (STRIP (BAG (STRIP (BAGA A 1
(SUBTRACT I 1))) (ACCESS A J) (STRIP (BAGA A (PLUS 1 I)
(SUBTRACT J 1))))) (STRIP (BAG (ACCESS A I) (STRIP (BAGA A
(PLUS 1 J) NN)) (STRIP (BAGA A J (SUBTRACT J 1))))))

207 LAMBDA INEQSTRIPBAG (LTQ (STRIP (BAG (STRIP (BAGA A 1
(SUBTRACT I 1))) (ACCESS A J) (STRIP (BAGA A (PLUS 1 I)
(SUBTRACT J 1))))) (STRIP (BAG (ACCESS A I) (STRIP (BAGA A
(PLUS 1 J) NN)) (STRIP (BAGA A J (SUBTRACT J 1))))))

The proof from this point will only be summarized, since it is lengthy but
uneventful. The goal is divided into nine subgoals by successive applications
of INEQSTRIPBAG. Each of these goals turns out to be easily proved, and the
proof ends successfully.

558 INEQIFTHENELSE = TRUE
559 INEQIFTHENELSE = TRUE
560
    TRUE

Acknowledgments

The work on program verification was done in close collaboration with
Bernie Elspas. The work on QA4 was done with Jeff Rulifson and Jan Derksen.
Irene Greif wrote the first version of the simplifier and participated in the con-
ceptualization of the pattern matcher and unification proofs. Jeff Rulifson encouraged us to write this paper and suggested its format. Rich Fikes has
helped with design modification and debugging of QA4. Bert Raphael read the
manuscript and suggested many improvements. Tony Hoare read and commented on the entire final draft; much of his advice was incorporated in the
published paper. This work has benefitted from our conversations with Cordell
Green, Peter Neumann, Larry Robinson, Earl Sacerdoti, René Reboh, Mark
Stickel, Steve Crocker, and John McCarthy. Many members of the Artificial
Intelligence Center and the Computer Science Group at SRI helped with support
and criticism.

The research reported herein was supported in part by the National Science
Foundation under Grant GJ-36146 and in part by the Advanced Research Pro-
jects Agency under Contract DAHC04-72-C-0008 and by the National Aeronau-
tics Space Administration under Contract NASW-2086.

Chapter 2
Logical Analysis of Programs

Shmuel Katz and Zohar Manna

1. Introduction

In recent years considerable effort has been devoted to the goal of proving (or "verifying") that a given computer program is partially correct—i.e., that if the program terminates, it satisfies some user-provided *input/output specification.* Floyd (1967) suggested a method for proving partial correctness of flowchart programs which has been shown amenable to mechanization [e.g., see King (1969), Deutsch (1973), Waldinger and Levitt (1974), Good et al. (1975), and Suzuki (1975)]. However, most existing implementations are incomplete in that they are not oriented toward incorrect programs: their declared goal is to prove that a correct program really is correct. If a program is not verified, it is unclear whether the program is erroneous or whether a proper proof has simply not been discovered.

We suggest conducting logical analysis of programs using "invariants" which express the actual relationships among the variables of the program. These "invariants" differ from Floyd's programmer-supplied "assertions" in that they are generated directly from the program text. In our conception, the invariants are independent of the output specification of the program and reflect what is actually happening during the computation, as opposed to what is supposed to be happening. Thus our invariants can be used either to verify the program with respect to its specifications or to prove that the program cannot be verified (i.e., contains an error). In addition, these invariants enable us to integrate proofs of termination and non-termination into our logical analysis. Invariants can also be used to debug an incorrect program, i.e., to diagnose the errors and to modify the program.

The need to relieve the user of the task of supplying fully detailed assertions (or invariants) has been widely recognized. We devote a large part of the paper to presenting techniques for the systematic generation of invariants.

Ultimately, we envision a system based on these techniques which would automatically generate the straightforward invariants. The programmer would still be expected to supply suggestions for those invariants requiring more insight into the logic of the program. Whenever new invariants had been produced, all invariants generated up to that point would be used to check simultaneously for correctness or incorrectness. If correctness (including termination) has been established, an attempt may be made to optimize the program through a fundamental revision of the program statements, based on the invariants. If incorrectness has been established, an attempt is made to automatically debug the program, i.e., to diagnose and correct the errors in a systematic manner, again using the invariants. If neither correctness nor incorrectness can be established, we attempt to generate additional invariants and repeat the process. Assertions ("comments") supplied by the programmer may or may not be correct, and therefore are considered to be just promising candidate invariants. As a last resort, it may nevertheless be possible to take a more radical approach and use the invariants for modifying the program so that correctness is guaranteed, taking the calculated risk of modifying an already correct program.

In the following sections we first present the techniques of automatic invariant generation, an algorithmic approach in Section 3, and a heuristic approach in Section 4. Then in Section 5 we describe the applications of the invariants for proving correctness (including termination) or incorrectness. In Section 6 we outline the practical implications of the invariants for automatic debugging. The Conclusion includes some bibliographical remarks.

2. Preliminaries

The programs treated in this paper are written in a simple flow-chart language with standard arithmetic operators over the domain of real or integer numbers. We assume a flowchart program P with input variables $\bar{x}$, which do not change during execution, and program variables $\bar{y}$, which do change during execution and whose final values constitute the output of the program. In addition, we are given an *input predicate* $\phi(\bar{x})$, which restricts the legal input values, and an *output predicate* $\psi(\bar{x}, \bar{y})$, which indicates the desired relationship between the input and output values.

For convenience we consider *blocked programs*. That is, we assume the program is divisible into (possibly nested) "blocks" in such a way that every block has at most one top-level loop (in addition to possible lower-level loops which are already contained in inner blocks). The blocks we consider have one entrance and may have many exists. Every "structured program" can be decomposed into such blocks.

The block structure allows us to treat the program by first considering inner blocks (ignoring momentarily that they are included in outer blocks) and then working outwards. Thus, for each block we can consider its top-level loop using information we have obtained from the inner blocks.

The top-level loop of a block can contain several branches, but all paths around the loop must have at least one common point. For each loop we will choose one such point as the *cutpoint* of the loop.

We use *counters* attached to each block containing a loop as an essential tool in our techniques. Since each loop has a unique cutpoint, we associate a counter with the cutpoint of the loop. The counter is initialized before entering the block so that its value is 0 upon first reaching the cutpoint, and is incremented by 1 exactly once somewhere along the loop before returning to the cutpoint. There are many locations where the initialization of the counters could be done. The two extreme cases are of special interest: (1) the counter is initialized only once, at the beginning of the program (a "global" initialization, parametrizing the total number of times the cutpoint is reached), or (2) the counter is initialized just before entering its block (a "local" initialization, indicating the number of executions of the corresponding loop since the most recent entrance to the block). In the continuation, we will assume a *local* initialization of counters, since our experience has been that this is generally the most convenient choice.

The counters will play a crucial role both for generating invariants and for proving termination. They will be used both to denote relations among the number of times various paths have been executed and to help express the values assumed by the program variables. It should be noted that it is unnecessary to add the counters physically to the body of the program. Their location can merely be indicated, since their behavior is already fixed.

It is sometimes convenient to add auxiliary cutpoints at the entrance and exit of a block. In addition, we always add a special cutpoint on each arc immediately preceding a HALT statement. Such cutpoints will be called *haltpoints* of the program.

A typical situation is shown in Figure 2.1. There is an inner block with cutpoint M and counter m, and an outer block with a cutpoint N and counter n. The outer block also has auxiliary cutpoints L and K at the entrance and exit of the block, respectively.

Our first task is to attach an appropriate invariant $q_i(\bar{x}, \bar{y})$ to each cutpoint i. We first define our terms.

A predicate $q_i(\bar{x}, \bar{y})$ is said to be an *invariant at cutpoint i w.r.t.* $\phi(\bar{x})$ if for every input $\bar{a}$ such that $\phi(\bar{a})$ is true, whenever we reach point i with $\bar{y} = \bar{b}$, then $q_i(\bar{a}, \bar{b})$ is true. An invariant at i is thus some statement about the variables which is true for the current values of the variables each time i is reached during execution.

For a path α from cutpoint i to cutpoint j, we define $R_\alpha(\bar{x}, \bar{y})$ as the condition for the path α to be traversed, and $r_\alpha(\bar{x}, \bar{y})$ as the transformation in the $\bar{y}$ values which occurs on path α. A set S of points of a program P is said to be *complete* if, for each cutpoint i in S, all the cutpoints on any path from START to i are also in S. For example, if L is the entrance to the program in Figure 2.1, $\{L\}$, $\{L, M, N\}$ and $\{L, M, N, K\}$ are all complete sets of cutpoints; $\{L, N\}$ is not.

We shall use the following sufficient condition [proven in Manna (1969)] for showing that assertions ("candidate invariants") are actually invariants.

Lemma A. *Let S be a complete set of cutpoints of a program P. Assertions* $\{q_i(\bar{x}, \bar{y}) \mid i \in S\}$ *will be a set of invariants for P w.r.t.* ϕ *if*

(a) *for every path α from the* START *statement to a cutpoint*

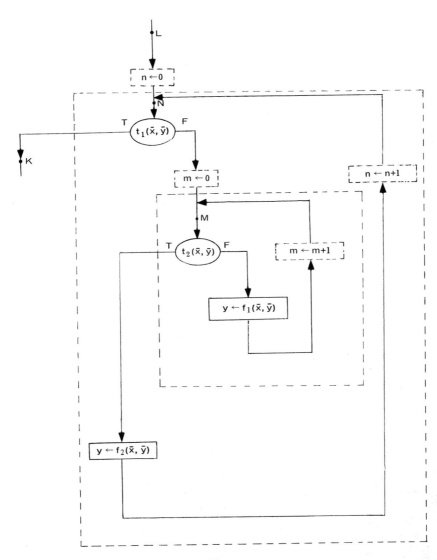

Figure 2.1. Blocks, Cutpoints, and Counters.

j (which does not contain any other cutpoint) [1] and

$$\forall \bar{x}[\phi(\bar{x}) \wedge R_\alpha(\bar{x}) \supset q_j(\bar{x}, r_\alpha(\bar{x}))],$$

(b) *for every path α from a cutpoint i to a cutpoint j (which does not contain any other cutpoint),*

$$\forall \bar{x} \forall \bar{y}[q_i(\bar{x}, \bar{y}) \wedge R_\alpha(\bar{x}, \bar{y}) \supset q_j(\bar{x}, r_\alpha(\bar{x}, \bar{y}))].$$

Consider, for example, the initial segment of a program shown in Figure 2.2. Assertions $q_1(\bar{x}, \bar{y})$ and $q_2(\bar{x}, \bar{y})$ will be invariants at cutpoints 1 and 2, respectively, if

(a) $\forall \bar{x}[\phi(\bar{x}) \supset q_1(\bar{x}, g(\bar{x}))]$,
(b) $\forall \bar{x} \forall \bar{y}[q_1(\bar{x}, \bar{y}) \wedge \sim t(\bar{x}, \bar{y}) \supset q_1(\bar{x}, f(\bar{x}, \bar{y}))]$,
    $\forall \bar{x} \forall \bar{y}[q_1(\bar{x}, \bar{y}) \wedge \quad t(\bar{x}, \bar{y}) \supset q_2(\bar{x}, h(\bar{x}, \bar{y}))]$.

Intuitively, condition (a) implies that $q_1(\bar{x}, \bar{y})$ holds the first time the cutpoint 1 is reached, while the first formula of (b) states that if $q_1(\bar{x}, \bar{y})$ holds at the cutpoint, it is still true after the loop is executed. Thus, by induction it follows that $q_1(\bar{x}, \bar{y})$ holds whenever cutpoint 1 is reached, i.e., it is an invariant at 1. The second formula of (b) states that if $q_1(\bar{x}, \bar{y})$ holds at cutpoint 1, then $q_2(\bar{x}, \bar{y})$ holds at cutpoint 2. Thus, since $q_1(\bar{x}, \bar{y})$ is an invariant at 1, $q_2(\bar{x}, \bar{y})$ is an invariant at 2.

Note that the input predicate $\phi(\bar{x})$, which depends only on $\bar{x}$ (variables not changed during execution), is automatically an invariant of any cutpoint of the program, and does not need any further justification.

Lemma A is slightly misleading, because it implies that a full-fledged set of assertions is provided at a complete set of the cutpoints and that these are checked simultaneously. In practice, the invariants will be added one after another until the needs of the logical analysis have been met. At every stage of the invariant generating process, a situation as in Figure 2.3 will apply for each block. At cutpoints L, N, and M, invariants $p(\bar{x}, \bar{y})$, $q(\bar{x}, \bar{y})$, and $s(\bar{x}, \bar{y})$, respectively will already have been proven. However, we also will

---

[1] Note that the $\bar{y}$ values are not defined at the START statement, and that they are initialized by constants or functions of $\bar{x}$ along a path from START. Thus, R_α and r_α for such a path are really only functions of $\bar{x}$, and not of $\bar{y}$.

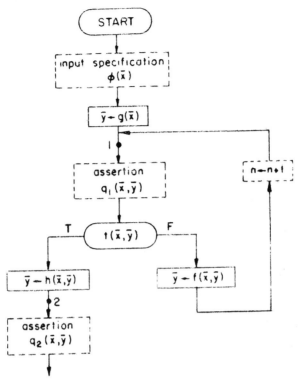

Figure 2.2. An Initial Segment of a Program.

have promising candidate invariants $p'(\bar{x}, \bar{y})$, $q'(\bar{x}, \bar{y})$ and $s'(\bar{x}, \bar{y})$, which we have so far been unable to prove invariant. These candidates could originate as comments given by the user or, as in the case of $s'(\bar{x}, \bar{y})$, from the output specification, which we automatically designate as a candidate at the haltpoints. As indicated in Section 4, additional candidates may be generated during this process.

For a block of the form given in Figure 2.3, we concentrate on developing invariants at cutpoint N on the loop. For the auxiliary cutpoint M, the invariants are generated by "pushing forward" any invariant obtained at N. Thus, if at any stage an invariant $q(\bar{x}, \bar{y})$ has been established at N, we automatically can take as an invariant at M any $s(\bar{x}, \bar{y})$ satisfying

$$\forall \bar{x} \, \forall \bar{y} [q(\bar{x}, \bar{y}) \wedge t(\bar{x}, \bar{y}) \supset s(\bar{x}, h(\bar{x}, \bar{y}))] \, .$$

To establish that a candidate $q'(\bar{x}, \bar{y})$ is actually an invariant at N,

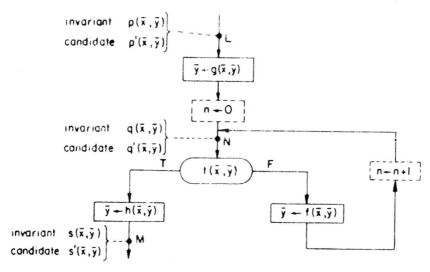

Figure 2.3. A Block Containing a Single-Path Loop.

it follows from Lemma A that we must show

(i) $\forall \overline{x} \, \forall \overline{y} [p(\overline{x}, \overline{y}) \supset q'(\overline{x}, g(\overline{x}, \overline{y}))]$

and

(ii) $\forall \overline{x} \, \forall \overline{y} [q(\overline{x}, \overline{y}) \wedge q'(\overline{x}, \overline{y}) \wedge \sim t(\overline{x}, \overline{y}) \supset q'(\overline{x}, f(\overline{x}, \overline{y}))]$.

It must be emphasized that special care should be taken in case of failure in an attempt to establish that a candidate is an invariant. For example, suppose that q'_1 and q'_2 are candidate invariants at the cutpoint N and that both q'_1 and q'_2 satisfy condition (i). It is entirely possible that neither q'_1 nor q'_2 satisfies condition (ii) individually, but that $q'_1 \wedge q'_2$ does satisfy condition (ii), and therefore is an invariant. This phenomenon—i.e., that it is impossible to show a weak property but it is possible to show a stronger one—is typical in mathematical proofs by induction. The explanation is that although we must show a stronger property on the right of the implication, we are also provided with a stronger inductive hypothesis on the left.

In Sections 3 and 4 we present techniques for discovering invariants. These techniques were originally designed with an automatic implementation in mind. However, they are in fact also useful for finding invariants by humans. For simplicity of presentation, we consider the single block of Figure 2.3. We will distinguish between two general approaches to producing invariants:

(1) the *algorithmic approach*, in which we obtain guaranteed invariants $q(\bar{x}, \bar{y})$ at N directly from the assignments and tests of the loop (using also any already established invariants at L and at N), and

(2) the *heuristic approach*, in which we obtain a new candidate $q'(\bar{x}, \bar{y})$ for an invariant at N from already established invariants at N and old candidates which we have not yet been able to prove to be invariants.

3. Generation of Invariants: Algorithmic Approach

We present first the algorithmic approach for generating invariants. We distinguish between invariants derivable from the assignment statements and ones based primarily on the test statements. The input predicate $\phi(\bar{x})$ and the fact that a counter is always a non-negative integer will be used as "built-in" invariants whenever convenient.

3.1. Generating invariants from assignment statements

We observe that assignment statements which are on the same path through the loop must have been executed an identical number of times whenever the cutpoint is reached. Thus the counter n of the cutpoint can be used to relate the variables iterated. We denote by $y(n)$ the value of y the $(n + 1)$th time the cutpoint is reached since the most recent entrance to the block (assuming a local initialization of the counters). Thus $y(0)$ indicates the value of y the first time the cutpoint is reached.

We use a self-evident fact as the basis for generating invariants: for $\bar{x}$ such that $\phi(\bar{x})$ is true and for each path α around the loop, we have

$$R_\alpha(\bar{x}, \bar{y}(n - 1)) \supset \bar{y}(n) = r_\alpha(\bar{x}, \bar{y}(n - 1)) \quad \text{for } n \geq 1. \quad (2.1)$$

That is, if values $\bar{y}(n - 1)$ occurred at the cutpoint, and a path α around the loop is then followed [that is, $R_\alpha(\bar{x}, \bar{y}(n - 1))$ is true], then the next values of $\bar{y}$ at the cutpoint [i.e., $\bar{y}(n)$] will be the result of applying r_α to $\bar{y}(n-1)$.

In practice, if there is only a single path around the loop such as in the block of Figure 2.3, it usually suffices to ignore the path condition R_α, and find invariants which satisfy the stronger condition

$$\bar{y}(n) = r_\alpha(\bar{x},\bar{y}(n-1)) \quad \text{for } n \geqslant 1. \tag{2.2}$$

Considering (2.2) for each component of $\bar{y}$, we have a set of recurrence equations, one for each y_j. We now attempt to express as many as possible of these equations in *iterative form*, e.g., as

(a) $y_j(n) = y_j(n-1) + g_j(\bar{x}, \bar{y}(n-1))$ or
(b) $y_j(n) = y_j(n-1) \cdot g_j(\bar{x}, \bar{y}(n-1))$.

Such forms are desirable because they can be solved to obtain

(a') $y_j(n) = y_j(0) + \sum_{i=1}^{n} g_j(\bar{x}, \bar{y}(i-1))$ or

(b') $y_j(n) = y_j(0) \cdot \prod_{i=1}^{n} g_j(\bar{x}, \bar{y}(i-1))$.

There are two ways to obtain invariants at a cutpoint from equations of the form (a') or (b'). First, it may be possible to express

$$\sum_{i=1}^{n} g_j(\bar{x}, \bar{y}(i-1)) \quad \text{or} \quad \prod_{i=1}^{n} g_j(\bar{x}, \bar{y}(i-1))$$

as only a function of $\bar{x}$ and n, not containing any elements of $\bar{y}(i-1)$. We then have an assertion which relates $y_j(n)$, $y_j(0)$, $\bar{x}$, and n. Second, if for two variables y_l and y_k there is a relation between

$$\sum_{i=1}^{n} g_l(\bar{x}, \bar{y}(i-1)) \quad \text{and} \quad \sum_{i=1}^{n} g_k(\bar{x}, \bar{y}(i-1)),$$

or between

$$\prod_{i=1}^{n} g_l(\bar{x}, \bar{y}(i-1)) \quad \text{and} \quad \prod_{i=1}^{n} g_k(\bar{x}, \bar{y}(i-1)),$$

then we can use this to connect $y_l(n)$ and $y_k(n)$. Once we have relations which are true for all $n \geqslant 0$, with all variables in the form $y_i(n)$, we can simplify by replacing each $y_i(n)$ by y_i, obtaining an invariant which may still contain occurrences of $y_i(0)$.

Whenever possible, known information from the entry invariant $p(\bar{x}, \bar{y})$ may be used to obtain $\bar{y}(0)$. When the variables are initialized immediately before entering the loop, $p(\bar{x}, \bar{y})$ will indicate the exact values of $\bar{y}(0)$. However, even when this is not the case, $p(\bar{x}, \bar{y})$ may often contain valuable information about $\bar{y}(0)$.

It is important to note that any predicate obtained as above, say from (a′) or (b′), is not simply a candidate for an invariant, *but is actually an invariant*. This is because substituting the correct initial value in place of $\bar{y}(0)$ ensures that the relation obtained is true the first time the cutpoint is reached, and the use of $r_\alpha(\bar{x}, \bar{y})$ in obtaining the recurrence equations ensures that the relation is true at subsequent times the cutpoint is reached.

Recall that the transformation from the recurrence equation (2.1) to (2.2) was made under the assumption that there was a single path around the loop as in Figure 2.3. The above discussion can easily be extended to the case of a loop with several possible paths–by using **if-then-else** expressions. For example, considering the loop of Figure 2.4, with two paths around the loop, Equation (2.1) expands to two equations:

$$\sim t_1(\bar{x}, \bar{y}(n-1)) \wedge t_2(\bar{x}, \bar{y}(n-1)) \supset \bar{y}(n) = f_1(\bar{x}, \bar{y}(n-1)),$$

and

$$\sim t_1(\bar{x}, \bar{y}(n-1)) \wedge \sim t_2(\bar{x}, \bar{y}(n-1)) \supset \bar{y}(n) = f_2(\bar{x}, \bar{y}(n-1)).$$

These can be combined into one statement, as

$$\sim t_1(\bar{x}, \bar{y}(n - 1)) \supset [\,\text{if } t_2(\bar{x}, \bar{y}(n - 1))$$
$$\text{then } \bar{y}(n) = f_1(\bar{x}, \bar{y}(n - 1))$$
$$\text{else } \bar{y}(n) = f_2(\bar{x}, \bar{y}(n - 1))\,].$$

Since $t_1(\bar{x}, \bar{y})$ controls the exit from the block, and does not affect the choice between the two paths around the loop, it can be ignored, as before, giving the stronger condition

$$\text{if } t_2(\bar{x}, \bar{y}(n-1)) \text{ then } \bar{y}(n) = f_1(\bar{x}, \bar{y}(n-1))$$
$$\text{else } \bar{y}(n) = f_2(\bar{x}, \bar{y}(n-1)). \tag{2.3}$$

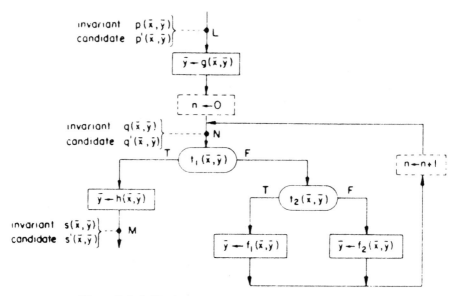

Figure 2.4. A Block Containing a Loop with Two Paths.

Equations of this form can then be put in iterative form, and treated just like equations of form (2.2).

3.2. Generating invariants from tests

So far we have concentrated on generating invariants from assignment statements, and the tests did not play a major role. Now we will show how the tests can aid in extracting additional invariants from the loop.

Suppose the block has the paths $\alpha_1, \alpha_2, ..., \alpha_k$ $(k \geqslant 1)$ from the cutpoint N around the loop back to N. Again we shall use an obvious fact: whenever N is reached during execution, either the block has just been entered, or control was previously at N and one of the paths $\alpha_1, ..., \alpha_k$ was followed. Letting n be the counter of the block, this can be written more precisely as

$$n = 0 \ \lor \ [R_{\alpha_1}(\bar{x}, \bar{y}(n-1)) \lor R_{\alpha_2}(\bar{x}, \bar{y}(n-1)) \lor \cdots$$
$$\lor R_{\alpha_k}(\bar{x}, \bar{y}(n-1))]. \tag{2.4}$$

This claim is clearly always true at N. By expressing $\bar{y}(n - 1)$

in terms of $\bar{y}(n)$ –using the recurrence equations given by (2.1)– and adding known information about $\bar{y}(0)$, we can often simplify (2.4). Again, if we obtain relations which are true for all $n \geq 0$, and all variables are expressed as $y_i(n)$, we can remove the parameter n to obtain an invariant.

We demonstrate some of the above techniques on a program. Note that we do not claim that this program is correct.

Example A.   Program[2] A of Figure 2.5 is intended to divide x_1 by x_2 within tolerance x_3, where x_1, x_2, and x_3 are real numbers satisfying $0 \leq x_1 < x_2$ and $0 < x_3$; the final value of y_4 is supposed to satisfy $x_1/x_2 - x_3 < y_4 \leq x_1/x_2$ at the haltpoint H. For clarity we have explicitly added the counter n to the program. There are two paths from the cutpoint N around the loop and back to N: the right path following the T-branch from the test $x_1 < y_1 + y_2$, and the left path following the corresponding F-branch. By using (2.1) we have for each path:

Right path:

$$[y_3(n-1) > x_3 \wedge x_1 < y_1(n-1) + y_2(n-1)]$$
$$\supset [y_1(n) = y_1(n-1) \wedge$$
$$y_2(n) = y_2(n-1)/2 \wedge$$
$$y_3(n) = y_3(n-1)/2 \wedge$$
$$y_4(n) = y_4(n-1)] .$$

Left path:

$$[y_3(n-1) > x_3 \wedge x_1 \geq y_1(n-1) + y_2(n-1)]$$
$$\supset [y_1(n) = y_1(n-1) + y_2(n-1) \wedge$$
$$y_2(n) = y_2(n-1)/2 \wedge$$
$$y_3(n) = y_3(n-1)/2 \wedge$$
$$y_4(n) = y_4(n-1) + y_3(n-1)/2] .$$

---

[2] This program is based on Wensley's (1958) division algorithm. Note that we use a vector assignment notation, where, for example, $(y_1, y_4) \leftarrow (y_1 + y_2, y_4 + y_3/2)$ means that $y_1 \leftarrow y_1 + y_2$ and $y_4 \leftarrow y_4 + y_3/2$ simultaneously.

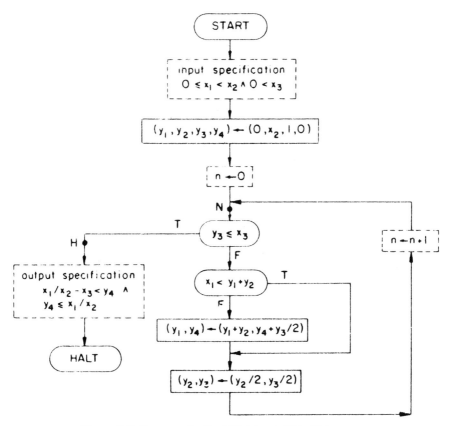

Figure 2.5. Program A. Real Division within Tolerance.

Since the assignments to y_2 and y_3 are not affected by which path is used, we may ignore the path conditions, obtaining

$$y_2(n) = y_2(n-1)/2 \;\wedge\; y_3(n) = y_3(n-1)/2.$$

Both of these are in the iterative form (b) and may be solved to yield

$$y_2(n) = y_2(0) \cdot \prod_{i=1}^{n} \frac{1}{2} \;\wedge\; y_3(n) = y_3(0) \cdot \prod_{i=1}^{n} \frac{1}{2}.$$

Since it is clear that $y_2(0) = x_2$ and $y_3(0) = 1$ at N and that $\Pi_{i=1}^{n} 1/2 = 1/2^n$, we have (dropping the parameter n) the invariants

(A1) $y_2 = x_2/2^n$ at N,

and

(A2) $y_3 = 1/2^n$ at N.

These may be combined to yield the additional invariant

(A3) $y_2 = x_2 \cdot y_3$ at N.

For variables y_1 and y_4, we apply the techniques used to obtain Equation (2.3): Ignoring the exit test $y_3 \leqslant x_3$ and expressing the effect of the branching by using **if-then-else**, the resulting recurrence relations are

$$y_1(n) = \text{if } x_1 < y_1(n-1) + y_2(n-1)$$
$$\text{then } y_1(n-1)$$
$$\text{else } y_1(n-1) + y_2(n-1),$$

and

$$y_4(n) = \text{if } x_1 < y_1(n-1) + y_2(n-1)$$
$$\text{then } y_4(n-1)$$
$$\text{else } y_4(n-1) + y_3(n-1)/2.$$

Both of these are in iterative form, and we can obtain the summations

$$y_1(n) = y_1(0) + \sum_{i=1}^{n} [\text{if } x_1 < y_1(i-1) + y_2(i-1)$$
$$\text{then } 0$$
$$\text{else } y_2(i-1)]$$

$$y_4(n) = y_4(0) + \sum_{i=1}^{n} [\text{if } x_1 < y_1(i-1) + y_2(i-1)$$
$$\text{then } 0$$
$$\text{else } y_3(i-1)/2].$$

We will use the invariant (A3), that $y_2 = x_2 \cdot y_3$ at N, in order to bring the two summations to an identical form. Substituting $x_2 \cdot y_3(i-1)$ for $y_2(i-1)$ in the **else** part of the equation for $y_1(n)$, factoring out x_2, and dividing by 2 inside the summation and multiplying by 2 outside, we obtain

$$y_1(n) = y_1(0) + 2x_2 \cdot \sum_{i=1}^{n} [\text{if } x_1 < y_1(i-1) + y_2(i-1)$$
$$\text{then } 0$$
$$\text{else } y_3(i-1)/2].$$

We have expressed $y_1(n)$ and $y_4(n)$ in terms of the same summation, which thus can be used to connect these two variables. Substituting $y_1(0) = 0$ and $y_4(0) = 0$, we obtain

$$y_1(n) = 2x_2 \cdot \sum_{i=1}^{n} [\text{if } x_1 < y_1(i-1) + y_2(i-1)$$
$$\text{then } 0$$
$$\text{else } y_3(i-1)/2]$$
$$= 2x_2 \cdot y_4(n).$$

Thus we have the invariant

(A4) $y_1 = 2x_2 \cdot y_4$ at N.

We now turn to Equation (2.4), using the tests of the loop to generate additional invariants. We have the fact

$n = 0$

$\vee \ [y_3(n-1) > x_3 \wedge x_1 < y_1(n-1) + y_2(n-1)]$ (right path)

$\vee \ [y_3(n-1) > x_3 \wedge x_1 \geqslant y_1(n-1) + y_2(n-1)]$ (left path).

For each path, we now use the equations for $\bar{y}(n)$ obtained from (2.1) to express $\bar{y}(n-1)$ in terms of $\bar{y}(n)$. For the right path we will use the fact that $y_1(n) = y_1(n-1)$, $y_2(n) = y_2(n-1)/2$, and $y_3(n) = y_3(n-1)/2$, while for the left path we will use the fact that $y_1(n) = y_1(n-1) + y_2(n-1)$ and $y_3(n) = y_3(n-1)/2$. These substitutions will yield.

$n = 0$

$\vee \ [2y_3(n) > x_3 \wedge x_1 < y_1(n) + 2y_2(n)]$ (right path)

$\vee \ [2y_3(n) > x_3 \wedge x_1 \geqslant y_1(n)]$ (left path).

Removing the parametrization in terms of n, and separating the term involving y_3, we have the two new invariants at N,

$[n = 0 \vee 2y_3 > x_3] \ \wedge \ [n = 0 \vee x_1 < y_1 + 2y_2 \vee x_1 \geqslant y_1]$.

To obtain stronger invariants, we can check whether the $n = 0$ case is subsumed in the other alternatives. The left conjunct may not be so reduced, and we have the invariant

(A5) $n = 0 \vee 2y_3 > x_3$ at N.

The $n = 0$ possibility in the right conjunct can easily be seen to be included in the other possibilities, since $y_1(0) = 0$ and $x_1 \geqslant 0$ imply that $x_1 \geqslant y_1(0)$. Thus we have the invariant

(A6) $x_1 < y_1 + 2y_2 \lor x_1 \geqslant y_1$ at N.

Note that invariant (A6) is a disjunction of the form $p \lor q$. This disjunction actually reflects the effect of taking the right path or the left path, respectively, around the loop. □

4. Generation of Invariants: Heuristic Approach

We now describe several heuristic techniques which suggest promising candidate invariants. There is no guarantee that the candidates produced are actually invariants, and they must be checked (using Lemma A).

It is important to notice that when we are unable to establish that a candidate is an invariant, it should be saved to retry later. In the meantime, additional invariants or new candidates may have been developed that, along with the original candidate, satisfy Lemma A.

It should be clear that before an automatic system for generating invariants is practical, strong guidance must be provided for the application of the following rules, since, applied blindly, they could result in too many irrelevant candidates. Here we merely state some of the various possibilities in order to give the flavor of this approach.

4.1. Disjunct Elimination

Whenever we have established an invariant at a cutpoint i which is a disjunction of the form

$$p_1 \lor p_2 \lor \cdots \lor p_k \qquad (k \geqslant 2),$$

we try to see whether any subdisjunction (in particular, each p_j alone) is itself an invariant at i. In the previous section, we actually used this approach when we eliminated the $n = 0$ alternative to obtain the invariant (A6).

4.2. Conjunct Elimination

Suppose we have at i a candidate which is a conjunction of the form

$$p_1 \wedge p_2 \wedge \cdots \wedge p_k \quad (k \geqslant 2),$$

and we have failed to prove that it is an invariant at i. One natural heuristic is to try a subconjunction (in particular, each p_j alone) as a "new" candidate. Note that the failure to prove $p_1 \wedge p_2 \wedge \cdots \wedge p_k$ an invariant says nothing about whether its subconjunctions are invariants. Theoretically, any nonempty subconjunction is a legitimate candidate and should be checked independently.

For the next three heuristics, we refer back to Figure 2.3.

4.3. Pushing Candidates Backward

Let us assume that $p(\bar{x}, \bar{y})$ is an established invariant at L and $q'(\bar{x}, \bar{y})$ is a candidate invariant at N. If the inductive step around the loop has been shown to establish $q'(\bar{x}, \bar{y})$ at N, then the only difficulty could be that $p(\bar{x}, \bar{y})$ did not imply $q'(\bar{x}, g(\bar{x}, \bar{y}))$. We then try

$$p'(\bar{x}, \bar{y}): \ q'(\bar{x}, g(\bar{x}, \bar{y}))$$

as a new candidate at L. This will "fix" the problem with $q'(\bar{x}, \bar{y})$, but of course we must now prove $p'(\bar{x}, \bar{y})$ an invariant at L. Note that in any case $p'(\bar{x}, \bar{y})$ must be an invariant at L if we are to succeed in showing that $q'(\bar{x}, \bar{y})$ is an invariant at N and in this sense is the "weakest" possible precondition for the base case of the induction for $q'(\bar{x}, \bar{y})$.

A similar technique can also be used to generate candidates at N:

Let us assume that $q(\bar{x}, \bar{y})$ is an established invariant at N and $s'(\bar{x}, \bar{y})$ is a candidate invariant at M. Since $s'(\bar{x}, \bar{y})$ is reached only from N, the reason we were not able to prove it an invariant must be that $q(\bar{x}, \bar{y}) \wedge t(\bar{x}, \bar{y})$ could not be shown to imply $s'(\bar{x}, h(\bar{x}, \bar{y}))$. Thus we would like to find a candidate $q'(\bar{x}, \bar{y})$ at N such that

$$[q(\bar{x}, \bar{y}) \wedge q'(\bar{x}, \bar{y}) \wedge t(\bar{x}, \bar{y})] \supset s'(\bar{x}, h(\bar{x}, \bar{y})). \tag{2.5}$$

Among the many possible choices of $q'(\bar{x}, \bar{y})$ which satisfy this condition are

$$q'(\bar{x}, \bar{y}): \ t(\bar{x}, \bar{y}) \supset s'(\bar{x}, h(\bar{x}, \bar{y})),$$

or $\qquad q'(\overline{x}, \overline{y}): s'(\overline{x}, h(\overline{x}, \overline{y}))$.

This first possibility is, just as above, the weakest possible assertion which satisfies (2.5), while the second is the strongest possible. A very useful third alternative to the above suggestions takes advantage of the transitivity of certain inequality or equality relations. For example, if we need a q' such that

$$q' \land B < C \supset A < C$$

where A, B, and C are any terms, then the relation $A \leqslant B$ is a natural candidate for q'.

Any candidate for $q'(\overline{x}, \overline{y})$ obtained from Equation (2.5) must be checked. Unfortunately, there are no clear-cut criteria for finding a $q'(\overline{x}, \overline{y})$ which will be easy to prove. If we fail to show some candidate $q'(\overline{x}, \overline{y})$ an invariant at N, some weaker version may nevertheless succeed. On the other hand, because of the "induction phenomenon", mentioned after Lemma A, it is quite possible that a stronger candidate $q'(\overline{x}, \overline{y})$ actually could be more easily proven.

4.4. Pushing Invariants Forward

Assuming that $p(\overline{x}, \overline{y})$ is an established invariant at L, a straightforward heuristic is to try to find a candidate $q'(\overline{x}, \overline{y})$ at N such that

$$p(\overline{x}, \overline{y}) \supset q'(\overline{x}, g(\overline{x}, \overline{y})).$$

The above equation ensures that the first time N is reached, $q'(\overline{x}, \overline{y})$ is true. Of course, in order to complete the proof that $q'(\overline{x}, \overline{y})$ is an invariant, the corresponding formula for the path around the loop must be considered.

Note that immediately after every assignment $y_i \leftarrow f(\overline{x}, \overline{y})$ where $f(\overline{x}, \overline{y})$ does not include y_i itself, we know that $y_i = f(\overline{x}, \overline{y})$ is an invariant. Also, after every text $t(\overline{x}, \overline{y})$ we can add the invariant $t(\overline{x}, \overline{y})$ on the T-branch, and $\sim t(\overline{x}, \overline{y})$ on the F-branch. Such invariants can also be pushed forward to generate useful candidates at the cutpoints.

4.5. Bounding Variables

One useful type of candidate for $q'(\overline{x}, y)$ at N is constructed by finding upper or lower bounds for the variables, expressed only in terms of *constant expressions* with respect to the block. That is, the bounds contain only constants, input variables, or other program variables which are unchanged inside the loop of the block.

Suppose that by considering $f(\bar{x}, \bar{y})$ and the invariant $q(\bar{x}, \bar{y})$ at N, we are able to identify a variable y_j which never decreases along the path around the loop. Now, if we can infer from $p(\bar{x}, \bar{y})$ an initial value $y_j(0) = E$ for y_j at N, where E is a constant expression with respect to the block, then we can conclude that $y_j \geqslant E$ is an invariant at N. Similarly, if y_j never increases, then $y_j \leqslant E$ is invariant.

A similar heuristic tries to establish that the variables maintain some data type, such as *integer* or *real,* during execution.

We will first illustrate the application of the heuristics in obtaining some additional invariants for the program of Example A, and then present a new example which will illustrate the possible interplay between the algorithmic and heuristic techniques.

Example A (continued). Let us consider again Program A of Figure 2.5. Applying the disjunct elimination rule of Section 4.1 to the invariant

(A6) $x_1 < y_1 + 2y_2 \lor x_1 \geqslant y_1$ at N,

we check first whether $x_1 < y_1 + 2y_2$ is itself an invariant. From Lemma A, we can show that

(a) $\forall \bar{x} [0 \leqslant x_1 < x_2 \land 0 < x_3 \supset x_1 < 0 + 2x_2]$ and

(b) $\forall \bar{x} \forall \bar{y} [x_1 < y_1 + 2y_2 \land y_3 > x_3 \land x_1 < y_1 + y_2$
$$\supset x_1 < y_1 + y_2],$$
$\forall \bar{x} \forall \bar{y} [x_1 < y_1 + 2y_2 \land y_3 > x_3 \land x_1 \geqslant y_1 + y_2$
$$\supset x_1 < y_1 + y_2 + y_2].$$

Since all of the conditions are true, we have the invariant

(A7) $x_1 < y_1 + 2y_2$ at N.

For $x_1 \geqslant y_1$, the second disjunct of (A6), we can show that

(a) $\forall \bar{x} [0 \leqslant x_1 < x_2 \land 0 < x_3 \supset x_1 \geqslant 0]$,

(b) $\forall \bar{x} \ \forall \ \bar{y}[x_1 \geqslant y_1 \ \wedge \ y_3 > x_3 \ \wedge \ x_1 < y_1 + y_2 \supset x_1 \geqslant y_1]$,

   $\forall \bar{x} \ \forall \ \bar{y}[x_1 \geqslant y_1 \ \wedge \ y_3 > x_3 \ \wedge \ x_1 \geqslant y_1 + y_2 \supset x_1 \geqslant y_1 + y_2]$.

Since these conditions are all true, we have shown that the second alternative is also an invariant, i.e.,

(A8) $x_1 \geqslant y_1$ at N.

We can combine the invariant (A4), $y_1 = 2x_2 \cdot y_4$, with (A8) and the input assertion $0 < x_2$ to obtain an upper bound on y_4 in terms of $\bar{x}$, i.e., the invariant

(A9) $y_4 \leqslant x_1/(2x_2)$ at N.

This invariant will be of special use later, in Sections 5 and 6, and in practice would be generated only when a need for such a bound arises.

Now, by pushing forward to H the invariants (A1) to (A9) at N, and adding the exit test $y_3 \leqslant x_3$, we obtain

(A10) $y_3 \leqslant x_3 \ \wedge \ y_2 = x_2/2^n \ \wedge \ y_3 = 1/2^n \ \wedge \ y_2 = x_2 \cdot y_3$

   $\wedge \ y_1 = 2x_2 \cdot y_4 \ \wedge \ (n = 0 \ \vee \ 2y_3 > x_3) \wedge x_1 < y_1 + 2y_2$

   $\wedge \ x_1 \geqslant y_1 \ \wedge y_4 \leqslant x_1/(2x_2)$ at H.   □

Example B. The program B shown in Figure 2.6 is supposed to perform integer division in a manner similar to computer hardware. For every integer input $x_1 \geqslant 0$ and $x_2 > 0$, we would like to have as output $y_1 = rem(x_1, x_2)$ and $y_4 = div(x_1, x_2)$, i.e., $x_1 = y_4 \cdot x_2 + y_1 \ \wedge \ 0 \leqslant y_1 < x_2 \wedge y_1, y_4 \in \{integers\}$. This program differs from the previous example in that it contains two loops, one after the other. The upper block, with counter n and cutpoint N, consists of a simple loop, while the lower block, with counter m and cutpoint M, consists of a loop with two paths. For convenience, we have added an additional cutpoint L between the blocks.

Our strategy will be to gather initially as many invariants as possible at N. The algorithmic techniques will be used to generate invariants at N directly, and then some of the heuristics presented above will be used to suggest additional invariants. We then push the invariants forward to cutpoint L, so that we have as many invariants as we

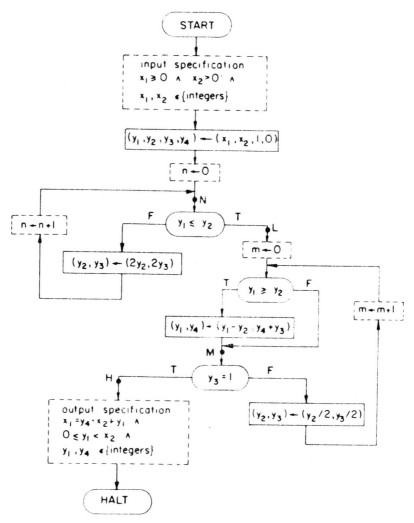

Figure 2.6. Program B. Hardware Integer Division.

can when the second block is first reached. Then we will employ the algorithmic techniques to generate invariants at M. Finally, we use heuristic techniques based on the invariants at L and M and the candidates implied by the output specification at H to generate additional invariants at M. We will not go into the problem of which heuristic rule to use first, but simply indicate how some candidates, which will indeed be useful invariants, can be found by using various heuristics.

Applying the algorithmic techniques for finding invariants at N, we obtain the equations

$$y_2(n) = y_2(0) \cdot \prod_{i=1}^{n} 2 = y_2(0) \cdot 2^n = x_2 \cdot 2^n \quad \text{at } N,$$

$$y_3(n) = y_3(0) \cdot \prod_{i=1}^{n} 2 = y_3(0) \cdot 2^n = 2^n \quad \text{at } N.$$

Thus we can obtain the invariants

(B1) $y_2 = x_2 \cdot 2^n \wedge y_3 = 2^n$ at N.

These can be combined to give

(B2) $y_2 = x_2 \cdot y_3$ at N.

By pushing forward the information in $\phi(\bar{x})$ and the initial asssignments (using the heuristic of Section 4.4), we get the additional invariants

(B3) $y_1 = x_1 \wedge y_4 = 0 \wedge y_1, y_2, y_3, y_4 \in \{\text{integers}\}$ at N.

Using the bounding variables rule of Section 4.5, we note that y_2 and y_3 are always increasing around the loop and, since $y_2(0) = x_2$ and $y_3(0) = 1$ at N, we obtain the invariants

(B4) $y_2 \geqslant x_2 \wedge y_3 \geqslant 1$ at N.

Note that (B4) could also be obtained directly from (B1) using the implicit invariant $n \geqslant 0$.

Using the T-branch of the test $y_1 \leqslant y_2$ and pushing forward to L the invariants at N, we have the invariants

(B5) $y_2 = x_2 \cdot 2^n \wedge y_3 = 2^n \wedge y_2 = x_2 \cdot y_3 \wedge y_1 = x_1 \wedge y_4 = 0 \wedge$
$y_1, y_2, y_3, y_4 \in \{\text{integers}\} \wedge y_2 \geqslant x_2 \wedge y_3 \geqslant 1 \wedge y_1 \leqslant y_2$ at L.

Generating invariants directly from the statements of the lower block, we first have the relations

$$y_2(m) = y_2(0)/2^m \quad \text{at } M,$$
$$y_3(m) = y_3(0)/2^m \quad \text{at } M.$$

Using the invariants $y_2 = x_2 \cdot 2^n$ and $y_3 = 2^n$ from (B5) to establish $y_2(0)$ and $y_3(0)$ at M, we obtain the invariants

(B6) $y_2 = x_2 \cdot 2^n / 2^m \; \wedge \; y_3 = 2^n / 2^m \; \wedge \; y_2 = x_2 \cdot y_3 \quad$ at $M.$

Using the same technique for y_1 and y_4, we obtain the recurrence relations

$$y_1(m) = y_1(m-1) + [\text{if } y_1(m-1) \geqslant y_2(m-1)$$
$$\text{then } -y_2(m-1)$$
and $$\text{else } 0] \qquad \text{at } M,$$
$$y_4(m) = y_4(m-1) + [\text{if } y_1(m-1) \geqslant y_2(m-1)$$
$$\text{then } y_3(m-1)$$
$$\text{else } 0] \qquad \text{at } M.$$

Writing these equations as a summation, then using (B6) to replace the occurrence of $-y_2(m-1)$ by $-x_2 \cdot y_3(m-1)$ and factoring out $-x_2$, we obtain

$$y_1(m) = y_1(0) - x_2 \cdot \sum_{i=1}^{m} [\text{if } y_1(i-1) \geqslant y_2(i-1)$$
$$\text{then } y_3(i-1)$$
and $$\text{else } 0] \qquad \text{at } M,$$

$$y_4(m) = y_4(0) + \sum_{i=1}^{m} [\text{if } y_1(i-1) \geqslant y_2(i-1)$$
$$\text{then } y_3(i-1)$$
$$\text{else } 0] \qquad \text{at } M.$$

Combining these formulas, we get

$$y_1(m) - y_1(0) = -x_2 \cdot [y_4(m) - y_4(0)] \quad \text{at } M. \qquad (2.6)$$

We will again use invariants from (B5) at L, namely $y_1 = x_1$ and $y_4 = 0$, to evaluate $y_1(0)$ and $y_4(0)$ at M. There are two possible paths from L to M. If the right branch is used, clearly

$$y_1(0) = x_1 \; \wedge \; y_4(0) = 0 \text{ at } M.$$

On the other hand, if the left branch is taken, the additional invariants from (B5), $y_1 \leqslant y_2$, $y_2 = x_2 \cdot y_3$ and $y_1 = x_1$ at L, together with the fact that $y_1 \geqslant y_2$ along this path, yield that $y_1 = y_2$ and $y_3 = y_2/x_2 = y_1/x_2 = x_1/x_2$. Therefore, after the assignments $y_1 \leftarrow y_1 - y_2$ and $y_4 \leftarrow y_4 + y_3$, we have that

$$y_1(0) = 0 \text{ and } y_4(0) = x_1/x_2 \text{ at } M.$$

Substituting both possibilities for $y_1(0)$ and $y_4(0)$ into the above equation (2.6), we obtain in both cases $y_1(m) - x_1 = -x_2 \cdot y_4(m)$. Thus we have the invariant

(B7) $x_1 = y_4 \cdot x_2 + y_1$ at M.

Turning to the tests, following Equation (2.4) we have

$\quad m = 0$

$\vee \quad [y_3(m-1) \neq 1 \wedge y_1(m-1) \geqslant y_2(m-1)/2]$ (left path)

$\vee \quad [y_3(m-1) \neq 1 \wedge y_1(m-1) < y_2(m-1)/2]$ (right path).

We try to substitute, using the recurrence equations for the left path in $y_3(m-1) \neq 1 \wedge y_1(m-1) \geqslant y_2(m-1)/2$, and the recurrence equations for the right path in $y_3(m-1) \neq 1 \wedge y_1(m-1) < y_2(m-1)/2$. For the left path, we have the recurrence relations

$$\left. \begin{aligned} y_1(m) &= y_1(m-1) - y_2(m-1)/2 \\ y_2(m) &= y_2(m-1)/2 \\ y_3(m) &= y_3(m-1)/2 \end{aligned} \right\} \quad \text{(left path)},$$

and for the right path we have

$$\left. \begin{aligned} y_1(m) &= y_1(m-1) \\ y_2(m) &= y_2(m-1)/2 \\ y_3(m) &= y_3(m-1)/2 \end{aligned} \right\} \quad \text{(right path)}.$$

Using these equations we obtain

$\quad m = 0$

$\vee \quad [2y_3(m) \neq 1 \wedge y_1(m) \geqslant 0]$ (left path)

$\vee \quad [2y_3(m) \neq 1 \wedge y_1(m) < y_2(m)]$ (right path).

Equivalently, we can write

$$[m = 0 \lor 2y_3(m) \neq 1] \land$$
$$[m = 0 \lor y_1(m) \geq 0 \lor y_1(m) < y_2(m)]. \qquad (2.7)$$

For the first conjunct, we can eliminate the $m = 0$ alternative because by (B5) we have $y_3(0) \geq 1$ at M, and therefore $2y_3(0) \neq 1$ at M. We therefore have the invariant

(B8) $2y_3 \neq 1$ at M.

For the second conjunct of (2.7), we can eliminate the $m = 0$ alternative because, as shown earlier, $y_1(0)$ at M is either 0 or x_1, and thus $y_1(m) \geq 0$ is true when $m = 0$. We have the invariant

(B9) $y_1 \geq 0 \lor y_1 < y_2$ at M.

So far we have used only the algorithmic techniques on the lower block, and have directly generated invariants (B6), (B7), (B8), and (B9) at M. Now we illustrate how some of the heuristic methods could be applied in order to obtain additional invariants.

Turning to the rule of Section 4.1, we consider each disjunct of (B9) separately. It is straightforward to show that both $y_1 \geq 0$ and $y_1 < y_2$ are invariants at M; i.e., we may add

(B10) $y_1 \geq 0 \land y_1 < y_2$ at M.

Using the rule of Section 4.4, we push forward to M the invariants in (B5), and among the candidates obtained is $y_3 \geq 1$. Since, using the invariant $y_3 = 2^n/2^m$ from (B6), we prove that for both paths around the loop

$$\forall \bar{y}[y_3 \geq 1 \land y_3 = 2^n/2^m \land y_3 \neq 1 \supset y_3/2 \geq 1],$$

we have the new invariant

(B11) $y_3 \geq 1$ at M.

(A consequence of (B11) is that $n \geq m$ at M.) In turn, (B11) can be used, along with invariants $y_2 = x_2 \cdot 2^n/2^m$ and $y_3 = 2^n/2^m$ from (B6), to show that the candidate $y_2, y_3 \in \{\text{integers}\}$ is an invariant.

We can obtain that $y_1, y_4 \in \{$integers$\}$ by pushing forward the invariants at L; thus

(B12) $y_1, y_2, y_3, y_4 \in \{$integers$\}$ at M.

Observe that if we had used the heuristic of Section 2.3 to push the given output specification at H backwards to M at an early stage, we could have obtained the important candidate invariants $x_1 = y_4 \cdot x_2 + y_1$, $0 \leqslant y_1$, $y_1, y_4 \in \{$integers$\}$, and $y_1 < x_2$ directly by this method. As shown, the first three candidates are indeed invariants at N, while any attempt to establish the fourth candidate $y_1 < x_2$ will fail.

Now, by pushing forward to H the invariants (B6) to (B12) at M, adding the exit test $y_3 = 1$, and simplifying, we obtain the invariants

(B13) $y_3 = 1 \wedge y_2 = x_2 \wedge n = m \wedge x_1 = y_4 \cdot x_2 + y_1 \wedge$

$\quad 0 \leqslant y_1 < x_2 \wedge y_1, y_2, y_3, y_4 \in \{$integers$\}$ at H.   □

5. Correctness and Incorrectness

As indicated in the Introduction, invariants may be used to prove the correctness or incorrectness of a program. In order to place these properties in their proper framework, we first present some basic definitions and lemmas [which follow Manna (1969, 1974)].

(a) A program P *terminates over* $\phi(\bar{x})$ if for every input $\bar{a}$ such that $\phi(\bar{a})$ is true, the execution reaches a HALT statement.
(b) A program P is *partially correct w.r.t.* $\phi(\bar{x})$ *and* $\psi(\bar{x}, \bar{y})$ if for every input $\bar{a}$ such that $\phi(\bar{a})$ is true, whenever the program terminates with some $\bar{b}$ as the final value of $\bar{y}$, $\psi(\bar{a}, \bar{b})$ is true.
(c) A program P is *totally correct w.r.t.* $\phi(\bar{x})$ *and* $\psi(\bar{x}, \bar{y})$ if for every input $\bar{a}$ such that $\phi(\bar{a})$ is true, the program terminates with some $\bar{b}$ as the final value of $\bar{y}$ and $\psi(\bar{a}, \bar{b})$ is true.

We are interested in proving that a program is either totally correct *(correct)* or not totally correct *(incorrect)*. We introduce termination and partial correctness because together they are equivalent to total correctness, and, as we shall see, for a proof technique based on invariants it is easier to prove these two properties separately rather than to prove total correctness directly.

The Lemmas B–D and B′–D′ (Table 2.1) use the invariants $\{q_h(\bar{x}, \bar{y})\}$ at the haltpoints to provide criteria for proving termination, partial correctness, total correctness, and their negations. For clarity we have used an informal abbreviated notation. Lemma B, for example, should be stated as:

Lemma B. *A program P terminates over ϕ if and only if for every set of invariants $\{q_i(\bar{x}, \bar{y})\}$ and every input $\bar{x}$ such that $\phi(\bar{x})$ is true, there exists a haltpoint h such that $\exists\bar{y}[q_h(\bar{x}, \bar{y})]$ is true.*

Proof. If the program terminates, then for every input $\bar{x}$ satisfying $\phi(\bar{x})$ some haltpoint h must be reached, and $\bar{y}$ will naturally have some value $\bar{b}$ at h. Then, by the definition of an invariant, for every set of invariants, $q_h(\bar{x}, \bar{b})$ must be true, i.e., $\exists\bar{y}[q_h(\bar{x}, \bar{y})]$ is true.

In order to prove the Lemma B in the other direction, we introduce the notion of a *minimal invariant* at cutpoint i, denoted by $m_i(\bar{x}, \bar{y})$. A minimal invariant $m_i(\bar{a}, \bar{b})$ is true for some input $\bar{a}$ satisfying $\phi(\bar{a})$ and for some $\bar{b}$ *if and only if* during execution with input $\bar{a}$ the cutpoint i is reached with $\bar{y} = \bar{b}$. Thus $m_i(\bar{x}, \bar{y})$ denotes the *exact domain* of the $\bar{y}$ values which occur at i during execution of the program with input $\bar{x}$.[3]

Now we assume that for every set of invariants and every $\bar{x}$ such that $\phi(\bar{x})$ is true, there exists a haltpoint h such that $\exists\bar{y}[q_h(\bar{x}, \bar{y})]$ is true. Then, in particular, this is true for the set of minimal invariants. By the definition of minimal invariant, since there exists a $\bar{y}$ such that $m_h(\bar{x}, \bar{y})$ is true, that $\bar{y}$ value actually occurs during execution at the haltpoint h, i.e., h must be reached, and the program must therefore terminate. □

The other lemmas may be proved by using similar arguments.

The six lemmas of Table 2.1 can be divided into two groups. The first group, Lemmas B′, C, and D′, are expressed in terms of the existence of a single set of invariants $\{q_i(\bar{x}, \bar{y})\}$ (an "$\exists\bar{q}$ formula"). They therefore may be used to prove nontermination, partial correct-

---

[3] Note that from its definition $m_i(\bar{x}, \bar{y})$ always exists as a predicate; for our purposes it is irrelevant how this predicate is expressed.

TABLE 2.1
Applications of the Invariants $\{q_i(\bar{x}, \bar{y})\}$

Lemma B. P terminates over ϕ if and only if
$$\forall \bar{q} \forall \bar{x} \exists h \exists \bar{y} [q_h(\bar{x}, \bar{y})].$$

Lemma B'. P does not terminate over ϕ if and only if
$$\exists \bar{q} \exists \bar{x} \forall h \forall \bar{y} [\sim q_h(\bar{x}, \bar{y})].$$

Lemma C. P is partially correct w.r.t. ϕ and ψ if and only if
$$\exists \bar{q} \forall \bar{x} \forall h \forall \bar{y} [q_h(\bar{x}, \bar{y}) \supset \psi(\bar{x}, \bar{y})].$$

Lemma C'. P is not partially correct w.r.t. ϕ and ψ if and only if
$$\forall \bar{q} \exists \bar{x} \exists h \exists \bar{y} [q_h(\bar{x}, \bar{y}) \wedge \sim \psi(\bar{x}, \bar{y})].$$

Lemma D. P is (totally) correct w.r.t. ϕ and ψ if and only if
$$\forall \bar{q} \forall \bar{x} \exists h \exists \bar{y} [q_h(\bar{x}, \bar{y}) \wedge \psi(\bar{x}, \bar{y})].$$

Lemma D'. P is incorrect w.r.t. ϕ and ψ if and only if
$$\exists \bar{q} \exists \bar{x} \forall h \forall \bar{y} [q_h(\bar{x}, \bar{y}) \supset \sim \psi(\bar{x}, \bar{y})].$$

$\forall \bar{q}$ means "for every set of invariants $\{q_i(\bar{x}, \bar{y})\}$".
$\exists \bar{q}$ means "there exists a set of invariants $\{q_i(\bar{x}, \bar{y})\}$".
$\forall \bar{x}$ means "for every input $\bar{x}$ such that $\phi(\bar{x})$ is true."
$\exists \bar{x}$ means "there exists an input $\bar{x}$ such that $\phi(\bar{x})$ is true".
$\forall h$ means "for every haltpoint h".
$\exists h$ means "there exists a haltpoint h".

---

ness, and incorrectness, respectively, by demonstrating a set of invariants which satisfies the appropriate formula. The techniques of Sections 3 and 4 can be used to produce such a set of invariants. Lemmas B, C', and D, on the other hand, are expressed in terms of every possible set of invariants $\{q_i(\bar{x}, \bar{y})\}$ (a "$\forall \bar{q}$ formula"), and may not be used directly with our techniques.

Since total correctness is expressed by a $\forall \bar{q}$ formula, we try to prove this property by showing partial correctness and termination separately. Lemma C uses an $\exists \bar{q}$ formula, and therefore is used to prove partial correctness. This lemma in fact represents "Floyd's method" for proving partial correctness. The problem of termination, however, remains, since it is expressed in terms of a $\forall \bar{q}$ formula. Termination must therefore be treated by other means, which will be discussed at the end of this section.

Incorrectness, on the other hand, is expressed by an $\exists \bar{q}$ formula, and therefore can be proven directly by our techniques, using Lemma D'. Note that the formula of this lemma can be expressed alternatively as

$$\exists \bar{q} \exists \bar{x} \forall h \forall \bar{y} [\sim q_h(\bar{x}, \bar{y}) \vee \sim \psi(\bar{x}, \bar{y})],$$

i.e., for some input $\bar{x}$, either the program does not terminate or the final result is incorrect.

We first illustrate the use of Lemma C for proving partial correctness.

Example B (continued). We would like to show that program B of Figure 2.6 is partially correct w.r.t.

$$\phi(\bar{x}) : x_1 \geqslant 0 \wedge x_2 > 0 \wedge x_1, x_2 \in \{\text{integers}\},$$
and

$$\psi(\bar{x}, \bar{y}) : x_1 = y_4 \cdot x_2 + y_1 \wedge 0 \leqslant y_1 < x_2 \wedge y_1, y_4 \in \{\text{integers}\}.$$

Using invariants (B1) to (B4) at N, (B5) at L, and (B6) to (B12) at M, we have established the invariants (B13) at H (the only haltpoint of the program). Since (B13) contains the invariants

$$x_1 = y_4 \cdot x_2 + y_1 \wedge 0 \leqslant y_1 < x_2 \wedge y_1, y_4 \in \{\text{integers}\},$$

we clearly have that

$$\forall \bar{x} \forall \bar{y} [q_H(\bar{x}, \bar{y}) \supset \psi(\bar{x}, \bar{y})].$$

Thus, by Lemma C, program B is partially correct w.r.t. ϕ and ψ. (Note that (B13) actually contains additional information about the final values of the variables, namely that $y_3 = 1$, $y_2 = x_2$, and $n = m$ at the haltpoint H.)   □

Thus, to prove partial correctness, we merely exhibit the invariants at the haltpoints which fulfill Lemma C. On the other hand, in order to prove incorrectness we must provide, in addition to appropriate invariants, an input value $\bar{x}_0$ satisfying $\phi(\bar{x}_0)$ such that the formula in Lemma D' is true. We would like to develop candidates for $\bar{x}_0$ in a systematic manner, similar to the way invariants were generated in Sections 3 and 4. For this reason, it is desirable to find a predicate $\phi'(\bar{x})$ which specifies a nonempty subset of the legal inputs for which the program is incorrect, rather than merely demonstrating the incorrectness for a single $\bar{x}$. That is, to establish incorrectness we prove that for some $\phi'(\bar{x})$,

$$\forall \bar{x} [\phi'(\bar{x}) \supset \phi(\bar{x})] \wedge$$
$$\exists \bar{x} \phi'(\bar{x}) \wedge$$
$$\exists \bar{q} \forall \bar{x} \forall h \forall \bar{y} [\phi'(\bar{x}) \wedge q_h(\bar{x}, \bar{y}) \supset \sim \psi(\bar{x}, \bar{y})].$$

In general, a proof which establishes incorrectness for a large set of input values is also more useful for the diagnosis and correction of the logical errors than an incorrectness proof for a single input value (see Section 6).

We will develop candidates for $\phi'(\bar{x})$ by starting with $\phi(\bar{x})$ and adding conjuncts (restrictions) to $\phi(\bar{x})$ one after another as the need arises. Thus $\phi'(\bar{x}) \supset \phi(\bar{x})$ will be guaranteed true. In case there are several alternative restrictions at some stage of the process, we prefer adding the weakest possible, so that $\phi'(\bar{x})$ will allow maximal freedom in choosing additional restrictions later. At each stage, of course, it is necessary to demonstrate that $\phi'(\bar{x})$ is satisfiable.

Note that all invariants which have been proven for $\phi(\bar{x})$ will remain true for any $\phi'(\bar{x})$ specifying a subset of $\phi(\bar{x})$. Moreover, at each stage of the process we now may discover additional invariants which are true for every $\bar{x}$ satisfying $\phi'(\bar{x})$ but are not necessarily true for every $\bar{x}$ satisfying $\phi(\bar{x})$.

Example A (continued). An attempt to prove the partial correctness of program A (Figure 2.5) will not succeed. Although the invariants (A10) at H can be used to establish $y_4 \leqslant x_1/x_2$ because

$$\forall \bar{x} \forall \bar{y} [y_4 \leqslant x_1/(2x_2) \supset y_4 \leqslant x_1/x_2],$$

we are unable to establish $x_1/x_2 - x_3 < y_4$. Thus we turn to incorrectness, trying to show that for some $\phi'(\bar{x})$ which specifies a nonempty subset of the legal inputs, and for some invariants $q_H(\bar{x}, \bar{y})$ at H, we have

$$\forall \bar{x} \forall \bar{y} [\phi'(\bar{x}) \wedge q_H(\bar{x}, \bar{y}) \supset x_1/x_2 - x_3 \geqslant y_4].$$

We first could try to show that the program is incorrect for *every* legal input $\bar{x}$, i.e., let $\phi'(\bar{x})$ be $\phi(\bar{x})$ itself, but such an attempt will fail. To find a better candidate $\phi'(\bar{x})$, we notice that the "desired" conjunct is $y_4 \leqslant x_1/x_2 - x_3$, and that the invariant $y_4 \leqslant x_1/(2x_2)$ at H of (A10) also provides an upper bound of y_4 in terms of $\bar{x}$. This suggests using the transitivity of inequalities to find an $r(\bar{x})$ such that

$$[y_4 \leqslant x_1/(2x_2) \wedge r(\bar{x})] \supset y_4 \leqslant x_1/x_2 - x_3.$$

The "most general" candidate for $r(\bar{x})$ is clearly $x_1/(2x_2) \leqslant x_1/x_2 - x_3$, or, equivalently,

$$r(\bar{x}) : x_3 \leqslant x_1/(2x_2).$$

The trial $\phi'(\overline{x})$ will therefore be $\phi(\overline{x}) \wedge r(\overline{x})$, i.e.,

$$\phi'(\overline{x}) : 0 \leqslant x_1 < x_2 \wedge 0 < x_3 \wedge x_3 \leqslant x_1/(2x_2).$$

From the development of $\phi'(\overline{x})$, it is obvious that $y_4 \leqslant x_1/x_2 - x_3$ is an invariant at H for every $\overline{x}$ satisfying $\phi'(\overline{x})$. Thus to establish incorrectness it only remains to show that $\phi'(\overline{x})$ is satisfiable. Since we may first choose any x_1 and x_2 such that $0 < x_1 < x_2$, and then choose any x_3 such that $0 < x_3 \leqslant x_1/(2x_2)$, the satisfiability of $\phi'(\overline{x})$ is obvious.   □

Recall that we have not yet provided a practical method for proving termination. The difficulty arose from the fact that Lemma B of Table 2.1 requires proving a "$\forall \overline{q}$ formula". Therefore we clearly need a special method for proving termination.

The traditional method suggested by Floyd (1967) involved choosing a well-founded set $(W, >)$, where $>$ is a partial ordering having the property that there is no infinitely descending chain of elements $w1 > w2 > \cdots$ from W. For every cutpoint i, one must find a partial function $u_i(\overline{x}, \overline{y})$ which maps the elements of the variables' domain into W, and an invariant $q_i(\overline{x}, \overline{y})$ which serves to restrict the domain of u_i. A proof of termination requires showing that each time control moves from cutpoint i to cutpoint j (along a path which includes no other cutpoints and which is a part of some loop), $u_i(\overline{x}, \overline{y}) > u_j(\overline{x}, \overline{y})$. Intuitively, since by definition there is no infinitely decreasing chain of elements in any well-founded set, the proof implies that no execution path of the program can be infinitely long.

The use of Floyd's method entails choosing the appropriate well-founded set $(W, >)$, the functions $\{u_i(\overline{x}, \overline{y})\}$, and the invariants $\{q_i(\overline{x}, \overline{y})\}$. We will suggest an alternative method for proving termination which will be strongly oriented toward the use of invariants, so that we may take advantage of the techniques of Sections 3 and 4. We present the method briefly.

As explained in the Preliminaries section, it is assumed that we can divide the given program into blocks in such a way that every block has only one top-level loop (in addition to possible "lower-level" loops already contained in inner blocks). We treat the inner-most blocks first, and work outwards. Thus, for each block we can consider only its top-level loop (with a unique cutpoint), assuming its inner blocks are known to terminate.

We suggest proving termination of a block with cutpoint i and counter n (assuming that the inner blocks terminate) by finding invariants which will imply that n is absolutely bounded from above at i. That is, $n \leq c_i$ at i for some constant c_i. Therefore, the cutpoint cannot be reached infinitely many times during computation. Note that it is actually sufficient to show $a_i(\overline{x}, n) \leq b_i(\overline{x})$ where $a_i(\overline{x}, n)$ is an integer-valued function monotonic in n [i.e., if n increases in value, so does $a_i(\overline{x}, n)$]. We therefore state

Lemma E (termination). *A program P terminates if and only if there exists a set of invariants $\{q_i\}$ and functions $\{a_i\}$ and $\{b_i\}$ such that for every block B with cutpoint i and counter n,*

$$\forall \overline{x} \, \forall \overline{y} \, \forall n [q_i(\overline{x}, \overline{y}, n) \supset a_i(\overline{x}, n) \leq b_i(\overline{x})], \qquad (2.8)$$

where $a_i(\overline{x}, n)$ is an integer-valued function monotonic in n.

The practical importance of the above Lemma E is that we may use invariants which link n to the program variables to derive directly the appropriate functions a_i and b_i. Recall that in such programs, we have the "built-in" invariant that n is a strictly increasing nonnegative integer. We shall use these properties in our examples without explicit indication. Although n and $a_i(\overline{x}, n)$ are integers, $b_i(\overline{x})$ can be any number, and the input variables $\overline{x}$ and program variables $\overline{y}$ need not even be numeric; this technique is perfectly applicable to programs with lists, strings, etc. Lemma E can be proved formally by reduction to Floyd's method.

One can weaken the termination condition (2.8) of Lemma E in several different ways. For example, we can often generate $R(\overline{x}, \overline{y})$, the disjunction of the conditions for following a path from Cutpoint i around the loop and back to i in B. We may then use it in proving that the counter in bounded, since if $R(\overline{x}, \overline{y})$ is false, the loop will terminate anyway. Another possibility is to use in a_i and b_i all those variables of $\overline{y}$ (and all those counters), denoted by $\overline{y}'$, which are not changed in B. Thus it actually suffices to prove the weaker condition

$$\forall \overline{x} \, \forall \overline{y} \, \forall n [q_i(\overline{x}, \overline{y}, n) \wedge R(\overline{x}, \overline{y}) \supset a_i(\overline{x}, \overline{y}', n) \leq b_i(\overline{x}, \overline{y}')]. \quad (2.9)$$

Example A (continued). Consider again Program A of Figure 2.5. From $\phi(\overline{x})$ and invariant (A2) we note that $0 < x_3 \wedge y_3 = 1/2^n$ is an invariant at N. Thus since

$$\forall \overline{x} \, \forall \overline{y} \, \forall \, n \, [0 < x_3 \wedge y_3 = 1/2^n \wedge y_3 > x_3 \supset 2^n < 1/x_3]$$

is true, it follows by Lemma E that the program terminates over $\phi(\overline{x})$.

□

Example B (continued). Consider Program B of Figure 2.6. Using the known invariant (B1), $y_2 = x_2 \cdot 2^n$ at N, and $\phi(\overline{x})$, we obtain

$$\forall \overline{x} \, \forall \overline{y} \, \forall n [x_2 > 0 \wedge y_2 = x_2 \cdot 2^n \wedge y_2 < y_1 \supset 2^n < y_1/x_2].$$

Since y_1 is unchanged in the upper block, it follows by 2.9 that the upper block terminates.

For the lower block we use the invariants (B6) and (B11), $y_3 = 2^n/2^m \wedge y_3 \geqslant 1$ at M, and obtain

$$\forall \overline{x} \, \forall \overline{y} \, \forall n \, \forall m [y_3 = 2^n/2^m \wedge y_3 \geqslant 1 \supset 2^m \leqslant 2^n].$$

Since n is unchanged in the lower block, the termination of this block also follows by 2.9.   □

The reader should not be misled into assuming that proving termination is always as trivial as it seems here. The method of Lemma E is examined in greater detail (and presented with some nontrivial examples) in Katz and Manna (1975).

Note that the method of Lemma E, as well as Floyd's original method, is useful only for showing termination. If we want to prove nontermination, both methods are inapplicable (again, *all* possible q_i's must be checked). Thus Lemma B' should be used.

Another important side benefit of using counters lies in the information provided on the time complexity of the given program. By analyzing the invariants at the cutpoints, upper bounds may be obtained on the number of times the loops can be executed. It is sometimes feasible also to discover an invariant of the form $r' \leqslant n$ at a point immediately after the exit from the loop, thus yielding a lower bound on the number of times the loop will be executed.

Example A (continued). Using the invariants (A2) and (A5) of program A (Figure 2.5),

$$y_3 = 1/2^n \quad \text{and} \quad n = 0 \vee 2y_3 > x_3 \quad \text{at } N,$$

we obtain the upper bound $n = 0 \vee 2^n < 2/x_3$.

The exit test and invariant (A2) imply that

$$y_3 = 1/2^n \quad \text{and} \quad y_3 \leqslant x_3 \quad \text{at } H.$$

Therefore $1/x_3 \leqslant 2^n$ is a lower bound upon exit from the loop. That is, in this program the relations

$$n = 0 \ \lor \ 1/x_3 \leqslant 2^n < 2/x_3$$

are satisfied, and the exact number of executions of the loop can be computed as a function of the input.   □

Example B (continued). In order to obtain an upper bound on the number of executions of the first loop of Program B (Figure 2.6), we need to generate an additional invariant which was not needed previously. Using the technique for generating invariants from tests, we obtain

$$n = 0 \ \lor \ y_1(n-1) > y_2(n-1).$$

Since $y_1(n) = y_1(n-1)$ and $y_2(n) = 2y_2(n-1)$, the resulting invariant is

$$n = 0 \ \lor \ y_1 > y_2/2 \quad \text{at } N.$$

Using the invariants (B1) and (B3), $y_1 = x_1$ and $y_2 = x_2 \cdot 2^n$ at N, the upper bound $n = 0 \lor 2^n < 2x_1/x_2$ is obtained.

From (B5) we have

$$y_2 = x_2 \cdot 2^n \ \land \ y_1 = x_1 \ \land \ y_1 \leqslant y_2 \quad \text{at } L.$$

This gives a lower bound of $x_1/x_2 \leqslant 2^n$. Thus, for the first loop the relations

$$n = 0 \ \lor x_1/x_2 \leqslant 2^n < 2x_1/x_2$$

are satisfied.

Since $n = m$ at H by (B13), it follows that the second loop is executed the same number of times as the first.   □

6. Automatic Debugging

In this section, we suggest a method for debugging based on the invariants generated from the program. The technique we describe uses the invariants and information about how they were generated in order to modify the program systematically.

As explained in the Introduction, failure to prove correctness leaves us unable to decide whether the program is actually incorrect or has merely eluded our efforts to prove its correctness. Two different philosophical approaches to automatic debugging can be applied as soon as we are unable to prove correctness of a program.

Following what may be termed the *conservative approach,* we would insist on a proof of incorrectness before proceeding to modify the program. This is a reasonable view, and, as will be indicated below, a proof of incorrectness can aid in debugging. The method presented for proving incorrectness of programs was motivated by this approach.

However, proofs of incorrectness are often difficult to obtain, in particular for subtle errors, since the needed $\phi'(\overline{x})$ (a class of inputs leading to incorrectness) must be produced. Thus an alternative to the conservative approach, a *radical approach,* can also be justified. In this approach, we will "fix" the program so that a proof of correctness is guaranteed to succeed, even without having proven that the original program is incorrect. In effect, under this approach we modify a program we merely *suspect* of being incorrect, taking the risk of modifying an already correct program.

The basic debugging technique using invariants is common to both approaches. We shall first describe the technique as it is used in the radical approach. The slight differences which arise if the conservative approach has been used (i.e., if a proof of incorrectness is available) are pointed out later in this section. At the end of the section we briefly compare the two approaches.

For simplicity we will again deal with a simplified model: a single block having no inner blocks, with a cutpoint L at the entrance, N inside the loop, and M at the exit, as in Figure 2.3 or 2.4. In addition to the candidates produced and invariants proven for each cutpoint during the process of invariant generation, we assume candidates $s''(\overline{x}, \overline{y})$ at M which would guarantee partial correctness of the program were they actually invariants. For the case in which M is a haltpoint, $s''(\overline{x}, \overline{y})$ would naturally be the output specification itself.

To effectively use the invariants for debugging, it is necessary to record in an *invariant table* all the information required to establish each invariant, e.g., the rule applied, and precisely how the program statements and other invariants were used in its derivation. In addition, the uses of that invariant for proving other invariants must be noted. In general there will be an entire invariant table associated with each cutpoint. However, there is usually an essential difference in the complexity of the table for cutpoints on a loop, like N, and for those not on a loop, like M. All of the invariants at M, for example, will be obtained simply by "pushing forward" either invariants at N or the exit condition of the block. Thus below we concentrate on the more interesting case of the invariant table at N.

For clarity, we will use a more pictorial representation for the invariant table at N and arrange the invariants generated in the form of a directed acyclic graph (dag). We use terminology similar to that of trees, talking about the "ancestors" or "descendants" of an invariant, and of moving "up" or "down" the graph, and we refer to the graph as an *invariant tree*. We will have invariants from previous blocks given in $p(\bar{x}, \bar{y})$, the initial assignment statements of the block, and the statements of the loop at the top of the tree. Each invariant $q(\bar{x}, \bar{y})$ at N is the descendant of the loop statements, initial assignments, and other invariants used to establish $q(\bar{x}, \bar{y})$.

By examining such an invariant tree, we can see both how a desired change in any given statement will affect the various invariants, and (conversely) how a desired change in an invariant can be achieved by changing statements.

The basic steps in correcting the program are as follows (again referring to Figures 2.3 or 2.4):

1. Using the heuristic methods of Section 4, such as 4.3, generate candidates for invariants $q''(\bar{x}, \bar{y})$ at N which would allow proving the candidates $s''(\bar{x}, \bar{y})$ at M to be invariants, and thus would allow proving partial correctness.[4] It is also possible to generate candidate exit tests $t'(\bar{x}, \bar{y})$ or candidate exit functions $h'(\bar{x}, \bar{y})$ which would guarantee partial correctness along with the existing invariants at N. In the continuation, we discuss changing only the invariants at N, although similar considerations apply to changing the exit test or exit function.

---

[4] The possibility that the program is partially correct but nonterminating will not be treated in our discussion; actually it would lead to a correcting process similar to that described here.

2. Find actual invariants $q(\overline{x}, \overline{y})$ in the invariant tree which are "similar" to those candidates $q''(\overline{x}, \overline{y})$ which guarantee correctness. The precise definition given to "similarity" will have a direct influence on the kinds of errors which may be corrected, and there are obviously many possibilities. We here assume that two predicates are *similar* if they differ only in constant (non-zero) coefficients of variables, a constant term, or other minor perturbations in the relation involved, such as $<$ in place of $\leqslant$. When we have succeeded in finding invariants $q(\overline{x}, \overline{y})$ in the tree similar to candidates $q''(\overline{x}, \overline{y})$, the candidates will be called the *goal candidates* at N, and denoted $q^*(\overline{x}, \overline{y})$.

3. Attempt to replace $q(\overline{x}, \overline{y})$ by the similar goal candidates $q^*(\overline{x}, \overline{y})$, moving up the tree and modifying the ancestors of $q(\overline{x}, \overline{y})$ so that the new $q^*(\overline{x}, \overline{y})$ will be derived rather than the former $q(\overline{x}, y)$.

4. When a *statement* has been modified in order to allow deriving a goal candidate, inspect (by moving down the tree) the effect of the modification on all other invariants derived from it. This is necessary in order to ensure that no other part of the proof of partial correctness or the proof of termination is disturbed. The inspection could require making additional "compensatory" changes in other statements, or abandoning a possible change.

Example A (continued). Consider once again Program A of Figure 2.5. The invariant tree for the program is shown in Figure 2.7. For simplicity, we have merely listed the number of the rule which was applied to obtain each invariant, rather than including more information. A brief review of the generation of invariants for this example (in Sections 3 and 4) should make the tree clear [except for (A11), which should be momentarily ignored]. We have added the "termination" and "partial correctness" boxes at the bottom of the tree to emphasize which statements and invariants were used to prove termination (with bound $2^n < 1/x_3$) and partial correctness (w.r.t. $y_4 \leqslant x_1/x_2$). Recall that we were unable to prove partial correctness for $x_1/x_2 - x_3 < y_4$, the first conjunct of the output specification. In order to demonstrate the radical approach, we momentarily ignore the fact that in Section 5 we actually have proven this program incorrect.

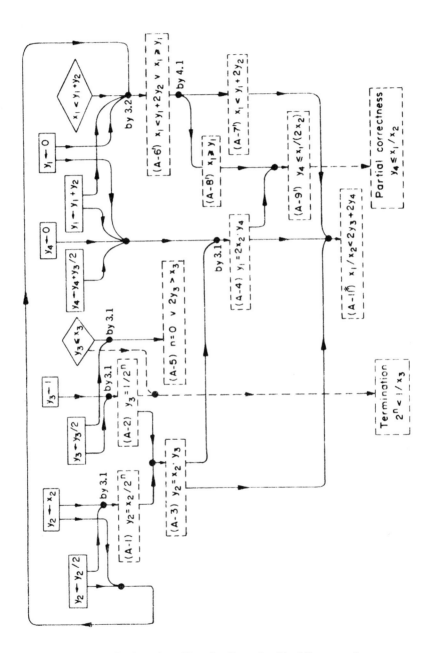

Figure 2.7. The Invariant Tree for Cutpoint N of Program A.

The problematic part of the output specification, $x_1/x_2 - x_3 < y_4$, is automatically a candidate invariant at H. Using the heuristic of Section 4.3, we can generate candidate invariants at N by pushing back the candidate at H (assuming temporarily that the exit test $y_3 \leqslant x_3$ is correct). The strongest candidate at N is $x_1/x_2 - x_3 < y_4$ itself. We may also use the transitivity of inequalities with $x_1/x_2 - x_3 < y_4$ and the exit condition $y_3 \leqslant x_3$ to suggest another natural candidate. We need a $q(\overline{x}, \overline{y})$ such that

$$q(\overline{x}, \overline{y}) \wedge y_3 \leqslant x_3 \supset x_1/x_2 - y_4 < x_3,$$

and see easily that the most general $q(\overline{x}, \overline{y})$ which will do this is $x_1/x_2 - y_4 < y_3$, or $x_1/x_2 < y_3 + y_4$.

Naturally, if either of these candidates could be proven to be an invariant at N, the program already would have been proven correct. Now we turn to the invariant tree in order to modify the program so that a correctness proof is possible. We look for invariants already in the tree which are similar to the above candidates, and also try to combine existing invariants into new ones similar to the candidates.

For the candidate $x_1/x_2 - x_3 < y_4$, we find no similar invariant. For the second candidate, $x_1/x_2 < y_3 + y_4$, we may combine (A3), (A4), and (A7), giving

$$[y_2 = x_2 \cdot y_3 \ \wedge \ y_1 = 2x_2 \cdot y_4 \ \wedge \ x_1 < y_1 + 2y_2] \supset$$
$$x_1/x_2 < 2y_3 + 2y_4, \qquad\qquad (2.10)$$

i.e., we have the new invariant

(A11) $x_1/x_2 < 2y_3 + 2y_4$ at N.

This is similar to the candidate, which we now will refer to as the goal candidate

(A11*) $x_1/x_2 < y_3 + y_4$ at N.

We have thus found a place to "hang" the candidate on the tree, and now must adjust the ancestors of (A11) [i.e., (A3), (A4), or (A7)] so that (A11*) will be derived instead. By examining Equation (2.10), it is not difficult to see that two of the most direct modifications among the many possibilities are

(a) leave (A3) and (A4) unchanged, but change

$$(A7) \ x_1 < y_1 + 2y_2 \ \text{to} \ (A7') \ 2x_1 < y_1 + 2y_2 \, ;$$

or

(b) leave (A7) unchanged, but change

$$(A3) \ y_2 = x_2 \cdot y_3 \ \text{to} \ (A3') \ 2y_2 = x_2 \cdot y_3$$

and

$$(A4) \ y_1 = 2x_2 \cdot y_4 \ \text{to} \ (A4') \ y_1 = x_2 \cdot y_4 \, .$$

Possibility (a) will be considered first. The invariant tree shows that (A7) was derived from the invariant

$$(A6) \ x_1 < y_1 + 2y_2 \ \lor \ x_1 \geq y_1 \ \text{at } N,$$

by using the Disjunct Elimination Rule of Section 4.1 to strengthen the invariant. To obtain (A7'), we will first modify (A6) to

$$(A6') \ 2x_1 < y_1 + 2y_2 \ \lor \ h(\bar{x}, \bar{y}),$$

where $h(\bar{x}, \bar{y})$ is the part of (A6') not of interest to us at the moment. By tracing back through the derivation of (A6) (which used the algorithmic rule of Section 3.2), the left alternative of (A6) can be seen to originate as

(i) $x_1 < y_1(n-1) + y_2(n-1)$

   (from the test $x_1 < y_1 + y_2$, using the right path),

(ii) $y_1(n) = y_1(n-1)$

   (from the fact that y_1 is unchanged along the right path),

(iii) $y_2(n) = y_2(n-1)/2$

   (from the assignment $y_2 \leftarrow y_2/2$).

These clearly were combined to yield the alternative $x_1 < y_1 + 2y_2$.

To obtain $2x_1 < y_1 + 2y_2$ instead, we replace (i) by $2x_1 < y_1(n-1) + y_2(n-1)$, i.e., change the test statement $x_1 < y_1 + y_2$ to $2x_1 < y_1 + y_2$. This suggested change was built to yield an acceptable left alternative of (A6'). Checking $2x_1 < y_1 + 2y_2$ alone, we may conclude that with this suggested change (A7') is indeed an invariant, and thus, so is the goal (A11*).

We must now check whether any other vital invariants are affected. From the tree it is clear that the only effect could be on the right alternative of (A6) and its descendants. Using the new test statement, it is easy to see that the left path leads to

$$2x_1 \geqslant y_1(n-1) + y_2(n-1)$$

$\qquad$ (from the test $2x_1 < y_1 + y_2$, using the left path),

$$y_1(n) = y_1(n-1) + y_2(n-1)$$

$\qquad$ (from the assignment $y_1 \leftarrow y_1 + y_2$ on the left path).

These clearly combine to yield $2x_1 \geqslant y_1(n)$, so that $h(\bar{x}, \bar{y})$ is $2x_1 \geqslant y_1$, and we have the invariant

(A6') $\quad 2x_1 < y_1 + 2y_2 \; \vee \; 2x_1 \geqslant y_1$ at N.

Examining the descendants of (A6'), we can see that (A8) must be replaced by

(A8') $\quad 2x_1 \geqslant y_1$ at N,

which is an invariant of the modified program. In turn, this combined with (A4) will yield the invariant

(A9') $\quad y_4 \leqslant x_1/x_2$ at N.

Thus we also have the invariant $y_4 \leqslant x_1/x_2$ instead of $y_4 \leqslant x_1/(2x_2)$ at H.

However, this invariant serves just as well as the original $y_4 \leqslant x_1/(2x_2)$ to guarantee partial correctness for the output specification $y_4 \leqslant x_1/x_2$. Thus the suggested correction leads to the goal (A11*)

and does not disturb any other aspect of the proof of correctness, i.e., the modified program is guaranteed correct. In Figure 2.8 we show the invariant tree at N of the modified program, which is totally correct. Thus, to summarize:

Replace the test $x_1 < y_1 + y_2$ *by* $2x_1 < y_1 + y_2$.

Possibility (b) for achieving the goal (A11*) will now be considered, i.e. we would like to replace (A3) and (A4) by (A3') and (A4'), respectively (again referring to the original invariant tree of Figure 2.7). We immediately note that since (A3) is an ancestor of (A4), any change in (A3) will influence (A4). The invariant (A4) was obtained by bringing two summations involving **if-then-else** to an identical form, so that y_1 and y_4 could be connected. If during the manipulations of the relations, $2y_2 = x_2 \cdot y_3$ is used for substitution instead of $y_2 = x_2 \cdot y_3$, the new (A4) becomes exactly $y_1 = x_2 \cdot y_4$, i.e., the (A4') we require. Thus if we can change (A3) to (A3'), we "automatically" have changed (A4) to (A4').

Examining the invariant tree, it is clear that we may achieve (A3') by changing either (A1) or (A2), i.e., either

(A1) $y_2 = x_2/2^n$ to (A1') $y_2 = x_2/2^{n+1}$

or

(A2) $y_3 = 1/2^n$ to (A2') $y_3 = 2/2^n$.

Since $y_2 = y_2(0)/2^n$ and $y_2(0) = x_2$, the first possibility can be achieved by letting $y_2(0) = x_2/2$, i.e., by changing the initialization $y_2 \leftarrow x_2$ to $y_2 \leftarrow x_2/2$. Now we check the possible effect of this change on other invariants. This initialization was used to establish (A6) and (A7) the first time N is reached, but the new initialization also does the same job. Tracing other paths down from this suggested change, we see that (A4) was used to establish $y_4 \leqslant x_1/(2x_2)$ at H. However, the new (A4'), $y_1 = x_2 \cdot y_4$, may still be combined with (A8), $y_1 \leqslant x_1$, to show that $y_4 \leqslant x_1/x_2$ at N and thus at H. Therefore this change is also safe, and we have

Replace the initialization $y_2 \leftarrow x_2$ *by* $y_2 \leftarrow x_2/2$.

The change in (A2), from $y_3 = 1/2^n$ to $y_3 = 2/2^n$, is also easy to achieve, since $y_3 = y_3(0)/2^n$. Thus we set $y_3(0) = 2$ instead of

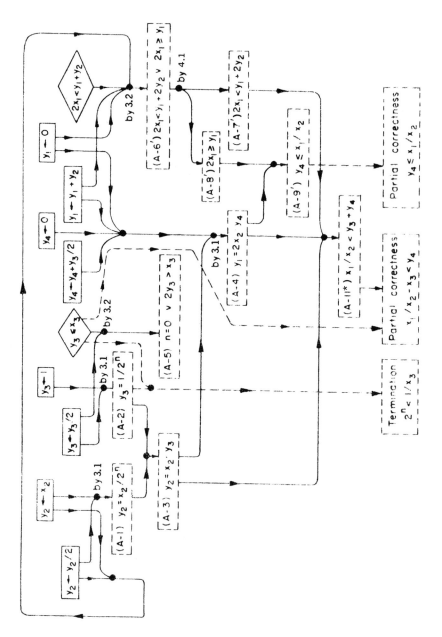

Figure 2.8. The Invariant Tree for Cutpoint N of the
Modified Program A (correction 1).

$y_3(0) = 1$, i.e., change the initialization $y_3 \leftarrow 1$ to $y_3 \leftarrow 2$. This change will slightly affect the termination, but the counter n can now be bounded by $2^n < 2/x_3$. Again (A4') can be shown not to disturb the correctness for $y_4 \leq x_1/x_2$. Thus a third safe change is

Replace the initialization $y_3 \leftarrow 1$ by $y_3 \leftarrow 2$.   □

So far in this section, we have ignored the possibility that we have already proven the program incorrect. Now we briefly consider how a proof of incorrectness can aid in the automatic debugging process described above.

We assume that when unable to prove correctness, the conservative approach was followed and a proof of incorrectness was produced. Although the existence of this proof has surprisingly little effect on the basic debugging technique, it can be of some aid. Clearly, any change in the program which is intended to correct the error must change at least one of the invariants used in the incorrectness proof. Thus the paths up the tree from the goal candidate can be restricted to those which will influence invariants from the proof of incorrectness. This is valuable because one of the difficulties with the use of the tree is the need for further guidance in the selection of likely paths.

Example A (continued). Let us review the proof of incorrectness of program A of Figure 2.5. We used the invariant $y_4 \leq x_1/(2x_2)$ at H [one of the invariants of (A10)] to find an $r(\overline{x})$ such that

$$[y_4 \leq x_1/(2x_2) \ \wedge \ r(\overline{x})] \ \supset \ y_4 \leq x_1/x_2 - x_3.$$

This suggested taking $r(\overline{x}) : x_1/(2x_2) \leq x_1/x_2 - x_3$, since

$$[y_4 \leq x_1/(2x_2) \ \wedge \ x_1/(2x_2) \leq x_1/x_2 - x_3] \ \supset$$

$$y_4 \leq x_1/x_2 - x_3. \tag{2.11}$$

This $r(\overline{x})$ then led to

$$\phi'(\overline{x}) : 0 \leq x_1 < x_2 \wedge 0 < x_3 \wedge x_1/(2x_2) \leq x_1/x_2 - x_3$$

which was then simplified and shown to be satisfiable.

Now $y_4 \leq x_1/(2x_2)$ at H was the only invariant used in the proof of incorrectness and was obtained directly from the invariant (A9), $y_4 \leq x_1/(2x_2)$ at N. Thus it follows that any correction of the program *must* change invariant (A9).   □

Let us briefly compare the two approaches.

Because we guarantee correctness, the "radical" approach of modifying without first proving incorrectness is not as dangerous as it might seem. In fact, the only objection would seem to be that in the case of a program which actually was originally correct, the efficiency of execution may be reduced in a modified (also correct) version. From our experience with hand simulations, we believe that *if* we are able to find goal candidates similar to the invariants, the program is very likely incorrect, and it is worthwhile to follow the radical approach without first proving incorrectness.

However, for programs with a large number of errors (or a small number of very gross errors), it is unlikely that the required similarity will be found. "Gross" errors could actually be defined as those which lead to invariants completely irrelevant to a proof of the specification.

In any case, the proof of incorrectness would be a valuable aid to the user, even if an automatic correction could not be made. It provides what could be called *logical diagnostics* about the program. From the conjuncts of the output specification which were contradicted, the general effect of the error is obtained. From $\phi'(\bar{x})$, the user obtains a class of inputs for which the program is incorrect. Most important, from the invariants directly used in the proof of incorrectness, the user can identify the problematic relations in the program.

7. Conclusion

In this paper we have presented an overview of how invariants can be produced and used. The basic concept of an invariant is, of course, not new. We have, however, tried to present a new perspective which shifts emphasis from the limited task of verifying a correct program to the more general framework of logical analysis. From our point of view, invariants are independent entities which can be used for many purposes, of which proving partial correctness is only one.

Numerous improvements and refinements are clearly possible to the invariant-generating techniques presented. In particular, it is necessary to further guide the heuristics in Section 4, so that they will not be applied indiscriminately. For example, only when the need for an invariant involving certain variables has become evident, should candidates involving those variables be generated.

The general problem of generating invariants for a given program is unsolvable. Programs clearly exist with relations among the variables based implicitly on deep mathematical theorems which could not conceivably be rediscovered by any general invariant-generating algorithm.

In a practical implementation, the user would be encouraged to provide his own ideas about what the intermediate invariants should be ("comments"), and these will automatically be considered as candidate invariants. The system could also ask the user to provide suggestions as the need arises for invariants involving specific problematic variables with unclear relationships at a certain cutpoint. We expect that a reasonably sophisticated system based on the techniques presented here, with some aid from the user whenever necessary, could produce sufficient invariants to conduct the logical analysis of some nontrivial programs.

Several other efforts have been made to attack the problem of finding assertions which prove partial correctness. The earliest work was by Floyd (private communications, 1967) and Cooper (1971). Elspas (1974) was the first to consider using recurrence relations. Wegbreit (1974) has developed independently some rules similar to our heuristic approach, and a method using a "weak interpretation" of the program. Katz and Manna (1973) suggested additional heuristics to treat arrays. Greif and Waldinger (1974) also described a method for generating assertions which moves backwards from the output specification.

The idea of adding variables, such as counters, to the program in order to facilitate proofs of partial correctness or termination is not new. Knuth (1968) uses a "time clock" incremented at every statement to prove termination. Elspas et al. (1973) also discuss how such counters can be used in termination proofs. Other related work on termination is that of Cooper (1971) and Sites (1974).

The possibility of using a program verifier to debug programs was first discussed informally by King (1970). Sussman (1975) stresses the importance of systematically eliminating bugs in the context of program synthesis. An attempt to establish incorrectness by finding counterexamples was outlined by Floyd (1971) as part of his proposed system for interactive program writing.

In our presentation we have basically considered the debugging of a program with a single loop. For more complicated programs, with multiple loops, additional research problems present themselves. What we have introduced here is clearly just a first step toward the use of invariants in debugging.

Acknowledgment

We are indebted to Ed Ashcroft, Nachum Dershowitz, Barnard Elspas, Stephen Ness, Tim Standish, and Richard Waldinger for their critical reading of the manuscript.

Chapter 3
Knowledge and Reasoning in Program Synthesis

Zohar Manna and Richard Waldinger

1. Introduction

In this paper we describe some of the knowledge and the reasoning ability that a system must have in order to construct computer programs automatically. We believe that such a system needs to embody a relatively small class of reasoning and programming tactics combined with a great deal of knowledge about the world. These tactics and this knowledge are expressed both procedurally (i.e., explicit in the description of a problem-solving process) and structurally (i.e., implicitly in the choice of representation). We consider the ability to reason as central to the program synthesis process, and most of this paper is concerned with the incorporation of common-sense reasoning techniques into a program synthesis system.

We regard program synthesis as a part of artificial intelligence. Many of the abilities we require of a program synthesizer, such as the ability to represent knowledge or to draw common-sense conclusions from facts, we would also expect from a natural-language understanding system or a robot problem solver. These general problems have been under study by researchers for many years, and we do not expect that they will all be solved in the near future. However, we still prefer to address these problems rather than

This is a revised version of a previously published article by the same name which appeared in *Artificial Intelligence,* vol. 6, pp. 175–208. Copyright 1975 by North-Holland Publishing Company, Amsterdam. Reprinted by permission of publisher.

restrict ourselves to a more limited program synthesis system without those abilities.

Thus, although implementation of some of the techniques in this paper has already been completed, others require further development before a complete implementation will be possible. We imagine the knowledge and reasoning tactics of the system to be expressed in a PLANNER-type language (Hewitt, 1971); our own implementation is in the QLISP language (Wilber, 1976). Further details on the implementation are discussed in Section 5.1.

Section 2 of the paper gives the basic techniques of reasoning for program synthesis. They include the formation of conditional tests and loops, the satisfaction of several simultaneous goals, and the handling of instructions with side effects. Section 3 applies the techniques of Section 2 to synthesize a nontrivial "patternmatcher" that determines whether a given expression is an instance of a given pattern. Section 4 demonstrates the modification of programs. We take the pattern matcher we have constructed in Section 3 and adapt it to construct a more complex program; a "unification algorithm" that determines whether two patterns have a common instance. In Section 5 we give some of the historical background of automatic program synthesis, and we compare this work with other recent efforts.

2. Fundamental Reasoning

In this section we will describe some of the reasoning and programming tactics that are basic to the operation of our proposed synthesizer. These tactics are not specific to one particular domain; they apply to any programming problem. In this class of tactics, we include the formation of program branches and loops and the handling of statements with side effects.

2.1. Specification and Tactics Language

We must first say something about how programming problems are to be specified. In this discussion we consider only correct and exact specifications in an artificial language. Thus, we will not discuss input-output examples [cf. Hardy (1975), Summers (1976)], traces [cf. Biermann and Krishnaswamy (1976)], or natural-language descriptions as methods for specifying programs: nor will we consider interactive specification of programs [cf. Balzer (1972)]. Neither are we limiting ourselves to the first-order predicate calculus [cf. Kowalski (1974)]. Instead, we try to introduce specification constructs that allow the natural and intuitive description of programming problems. We therefore include constructs such as

$$\text{Find } x \text{ such that } P(x)$$

and the ellipsis notation, e.g.,

$$A[1], A[2], ..., A[n].$$

Furthermore, we introduce new constructs that are specific to certain subject domains. For instance, in the domain of sets we use

$$\{x \mid P(x)\}$$

for "the set of all x such that $P(x)$". As we introduce an example we will describe features of the language that apply to that example. Since the specification language is extendible, we can introduce new constructs at any time.

We use a separate language to express the system's knowledge and reasoning tactics. In the paper, these will be expressed in the form of rules written in English. In our implementation, the same rules are represented as programs in the QLISP programming language. When a problem or goal is presented to the system, the appropriate rules are summoned by "pattern-directed function invocation" (Hewitt, 1971). In other words, the form of the goal determines which rules are applied.

In the following two sections we will use a single example, the synthesis of the set-theoretic union program to illustrate the formation both of conditionals and of loops. The problem here is to compute the union of two finite sets, where sets are represented as lists with no repeated elements.

Given two sets, s and t, we want to express

$$union(s\ t) = \{x \mid x \in s \text{ or } x \in t\}$$

in a LISP-like language. We expect the output of the synthesized program to be a set itself. Thus

$$union((A\ B)\ (B\ C)) = (A\ B\ C).$$

We do not regard the expression $\{x \mid x \in s \text{ or } x \in t\}$ itself as a proper program: the operator $\{ \ | \ ...\}$ is a construct in our specification language but not in our LISP-like programming language. We assume that the programming language does have the following functions:

$head(l)$ = the first element of the list l. Thus $head((A \ B \ C \ D)) = A$.

$tail(l)$ = the list of all but the first element of the list l. Thus $tail((A \ B \ C \ D)) = (B \ C \ D)$.[1]

$add(x \ s)$ = the set consisting of the element x and the elements of the set s. Thus $add(A \ (B \ C \ D)) = (A \ B \ C \ D)$ whereas $add(B \ (B \ C \ D)) = (B \ C \ D)$.

$empty(s)$ is true if s is the empty list, and false otherwise.

Our task is to transform the specification for *union* into an equivalent algorithm in this programming language.

We assume the system has some basic knowledge about sets, such as the following rules:

(1) $x \in s$ is false if $empty(s)$.

(2) s is equal to $add(head(s) \ tail(s))$ if $\sim empty(s)$.

(3) $x \in add(s \ t)$ is equivalent to ($x = s$ or $x \in t$).

(4) $\{x \mid x \in s\}$ is equal to s.

(5) $\{x \mid x = a \text{ or } Q(x)\}$ is equal to $add(a \ \{x \mid Q(x)\})$.

We also assume that the system knows a considerable amount of propositional logic, which we will not mention expliticly.

Before proceeding with our example we must discuss the formation of conditional expressions.

2.2. Formation of Conditional Expressions

In addition to the above constructs, we assume that our programming language contains conditional expressions of the form

$$(\text{if } p \text{ then } q \text{ else } r) = \begin{cases} r & \text{if } p \text{ is false,} \\ q & \text{otherwise.} \end{cases}$$

The conditional expression is a technique for dealing with uncer-

---

[1] Since sets are represented as lists, *head* and *tail* may be applied to sets as well as lists. Their value then depends on our actual choice of representation.

tainty. Suppose, in constructing a program, we want to know if condition p is true or false, when in fact p may be true on some occasions and false on others, depending on the values of the program's arguments. The human programmer faced with this problem is likely to resort to "hypothetical reasoning": he will assume p is false and write a program r that solves his program in that case; then he will assume p is true and write a program q that works in that case; he will then put the two programs together into a single program

$$(\text{if } p \text{ then } q \text{ else } r).$$

Conceptually he has solved his problem by splitting his world into two worlds: the case in which p is true and the case in which p is false. In each of these worlds, uncertainty is reduced. Note that we must be careful that the condition p on which we are splitting the world is computable in our programming language; otherwise, the conditional expression we construct also will not be computable.

We can now proceed with the synthesis of the union function. Our specifications were

$$union(s\ t) = \{x \mid x \in s \text{ or } x \in t\}.$$

We begin to transform these specifications using our rules. Rule (1) applies to the subexpression $x \in s$, generating a subgoal, $empty(s)$. We cannot prove s is empty—this depends on the input—and therefor e this is an occasion for a hypothetical world split. (We know that $empty(s)$ is a computable condition because $empty$ is a primitive in our language.) In the case in which s is empty, the expression

$$\{x \mid x \in s \text{ or } x \in t\}$$

therefore reduces to

$$\{x \mid \text{false or } x \in t\},$$

or, by propositional logic,

$$\{x \mid x \in t\}.$$

Now rule (4) reduces this to t, which is one of the inputs to our program and therefore is itself an acceptable program segment in our language.

In the other world—the case in which s is not empty—we cannot solve the problem without resorting to the recursive loop formation mechanism, which is the subject of the next section. However, we know at this point that the program will have the form

$$union(s\ t) = \text{if } empty(s)$$
$$\text{then } t$$
$$\text{else}. . .,$$

where the else clause will be whatever program segment we construct for the case in which s is not empty.

2.3. Formation of Loops

The term "loop" includes both iteration and recursion; however, in this paper we will only discuss recursive loops [cf. Manna and Waldinger (1971)]. Intuitively, we form a recursive call when, in the course of working on our problem, we generate a subgoal that is identical in form to our top-level goal. For instance, suppose our top-level goal is to construct the program $reverse(l)$ that reverses the elements of the list l [e.g., $reverse(A\ (B\ C)\ D)=(D\ (B\ C)\ A)$]. If in the course of constructing this program we generate the subgoal of reversing the elements of the list $tail(l)$, we can use the program we are constructing to satisfy this subgoal. In other words, we can introduce a recursive call $reverse(tail(l))$ to solve the subsidiary problem. We must always check that a recursive call does not lead to an infinite recursion. No such infinite loop can occur here, because the input $tail(l)$ is "shorter" than the original input l.

Let us see how the technique applies to our union example. Continuing where we left off in the discussion of conditionals, we attempt to expand the expression

$$\{x \mid x \in s \text{ or } x \in t\}$$

in the case in which s is not empty. Applying rule (2) to the sub-expression s, we can expand our expression to

$$\{x \mid x \in add(head(s)\ tail(s)) \text{ or } x \in t\}.$$

This is transformed by rule (3) into

$$\{x \mid x = head(s) \text{ or } x \in tail(s) \text{ or } x \in t\}.$$

Using rule (5), this reduces to

$$add(head(s)\ \{x \mid x \in tail(s) \text{ or } x \in t\}).$$

If we observe that
$$\{x \mid x \in tail(s) \text{ or } x \in t\}$$
is an instance of the top-level subgoal, we can reduce it to
$$union(tail(s)\ t).$$

Again, this recursive call leads to no infinite loops, since $tail(s)$ is shorter than s. Our completed union program is now

$$union(s\ t) = \text{if } empty(s)$$
$$\text{then } t$$
$$\text{else } add(head(s)\quad union(tail(s)\ t)).$$

As presented in this section, the loop formation technique can only be applied if a subgoal is generated that is a special case of the top-level goal. We shall see in the next section how this restriction can be relaxed.

2.4. Generalization of Specifications

When proving a theorem by mathematical induction, it is often necessary to strengthen the theorem in order for the induction to "go through". Even though we have an apparently more difficult theorem to prove, the proof is facilitated because we have a stronger induction hypothesis. For example, in proving theorems about LISP programs, the theorem prover of Boyer and Moore (1975) often automatically generalizes the statement of the theorem in the course of a proof by induction.

A similar phenomenon occurs in the synthesis of a recursive program. It is often necessary to strengthen the specifications of a program in order for that program to be useful in recursive calls. We believe that this ability to strengthen specifications is an essential part of the synthesis process, as many of our examples will show.

For example, suppose we want to construct a program to reverse a list. A good recursive *reverse* program is
$$reverse(l) = rev(l\ ()),$$
where

$$rev(l\ m) = \text{if } empty(l)$$
$$\text{then } m$$
$$\text{else } rev(tail(l)\quad head(l) \cdot m).$$

Here () is the empty list, and $x \cdot l$ is the list formed by inserting x before the first element of the list l [e.g., $A \cdot (B\ C\ D) = (A\ B\ C\ D)$]. Note that $rev(l\ m)$ reverses the list l and appends it onto the list m, e.g.,

$$rev((A\ B\ C)\ (D\ E\ )) = (C\ B\ A\ D\ E).$$

This is a good way to compute *reverse*: it uses very primitive LISP functions, and its recursion is such that it can be compiled without the use of a stack. However, writing such a program entails writing the function *rev*, which is apparently more general and difficult to compute than *reverse* itself, since it must reverse its first argument as a subtask. Actually, the more general program *rev* is easier to construct, and the synthesis of the reverse function involves generalizing the original specifications of *reverse* into the specifications of *rev*.

The *reverse* function requires that the top-level goal be generalized in order to match the lower-level goal. Another way to strengthen the specifications is to propose additional requirements for the program being constructed. For instance, suppose in the course of the synthesis of a function $f(x)$, we generate a subgoal of the form $P(f(a))$, where $f(a)$ is a particular recursive call. If we cannot prove $P(f(a))$, it may still be possible to strengthen the specifications for $f(x)$ so as to also satisfy $P(f(x))$ for all x. This step may require that we actually modify portions of the program f that have already been synthesized in order to satisfy the new specification P. The recursive call to the modified program will then be sure to satisfy $P(f(a))$. This process will be illustrated in more detail during the synthesis of the pattern matcher in Section 3.

The recursion-introduction mechanism presented here has been developed independently by Burstall and Darlington (1977).

2.5. Conjunctive Goals

The problem of solving conjunctive goals is the problem of constructing an output that satisfies two (or more) constraints. The general form for this problem is

Find z such that $P(z)$ and $Q(z)$.

The conjunctive-goal problem is difficult because, even if we have methods for solving the goals

$$\text{Find } z \text{ such that } P(z)$$

and

$$\text{Find } z \text{ such that } Q(z)$$

independently, the two solutions may not merge together nicely into a single solution. Moreover, there seems to be no way of solving the conjunctive-goal problem in general; a method that works on one such problem may be irrelevant to another.

We will illustrate one instance of the conjunctive-goal problem: the solution of two simultaneous linear equations. Although this problem is not itself a program synthesis problem, it could be rephrased as one. Moreover, the difficulties involved and the technique to be applied extend to many real synthesis problems, such as the pattern-matcher synthesis of Section 3. Suppose our problem is the following:

$$\text{Find } \langle z_1, z_2 \rangle \text{ such that } 2z_1 = z_2 + 1 \text{ and } 2z_2 = z_1 + 2.$$

Suppose further that although we can solve single linear equations with ease, we have no built-in package for solving sets of equations simultaneously. We may try first to find a solution to each equation separately. Solving the first equation, we might come up with

$$\langle z_1, z_2 \rangle = \langle 1, 1 \rangle,$$

whereas solving the second equation might give

$$\langle z_1, z_2 \rangle = \langle 2, 2 \rangle.$$

There is no way of combining these two solutions. Furthermore, it does not help matters to reverse the order in which we approach the two subgoals. What is necessary is to make the solution of the first goal as general as possible, so that some special case of the solution might satisfy the second goal as well. For instance, a "general" solution to the first equation might be

$$\langle 1 + w, \ 1 + 2w \rangle \quad \text{for any } w.$$

This solution is a generalization of our earlier solution $\langle 1, 1 \rangle$. The problem is now to find a special case of the general solution that also solves the second equation. In other words, we must find a w such that

$$2(1 + 2w) = (1 + w) + 2.$$

This strategy leads us to a solution.

Of course, the method of generalization does not apply to all conjunctive-goal problems. For instance, the synthesis of an integer square-root program has specifications

> Find z such that
> z is an integer and
> $z^2 \leqslant x$ and
> $(z + 1)^2 > x$,
> where $x \geqslant 0$.

The above approach of finding a general solution to one of the conjuncts and plugging it into the others is not effective in this case.

2.6. Side Effects

Up to now we have been considering programs in a LISP-like language: these programs return a value but effect no change in any data structure. In the next two sections we will consider the synthesis of programs with "side effects" that may modify the state of the world.

For instance, a LISP-like program to sort two variables x and y would return as its value a list of two numbers, either $(x \ y)$ or $(y \ x)$, without altering the contents of x and y. On the other hand, a program with side effects to sort x and y might change the contents of x and y.

In order to indicate that a program with side effects is to be constructed, we provide a specification of form

> Achieve P.

This construct means that the world is to be changed so as to make P true. For instance, if we specify a program

> Achieve $x = y$.

we intend that the program actually change the value of x or y, say by an assignment statement. However, if we specify

> Find x such that $x = y$,

the program constructed would return the value of y, but would not change the value of x or y.

Many of the techniques we used in the synthesis of LISP-like programs also apply to the construction of programs with side effects. In particular, we can use pattern-directed function invocation to retrieve tactical knowledge. The synthesis of the program in the following example has the same flavor as our earlier union example, but involves the introduction of side effects.

The program $sort(x\ y)$ to be constructed is to sort the values of two variables x and y. For simplicity we will allow the use of the statement $interchange(x\ y)$ to exchange the values of x and y, instead of the usual sequence of assignment statements. Our specification will be simply

$$\text{Achieve } x \leqslant y.$$

Strictly speaking, we should include in the specification the additional requirement that the set of values of x and y after the sort should be the same as before. However, we will not consider such compound goals until Section 2.8, and we can achieve the same effect by requiring that the *interchange* statement be the only instruction with side effects that appears in the program.

The first step in achieving a goal is to see if it is already true. (If a goal is a theorem, for instance, we do not need to construct a program to achieve it.) We cannot prove $x \leqslant y$, but we can use it as a basis for a hypothetical world split. This split corresponds to a conditional expression in the program being constructed. In flow-chart notation the conditional expression is written as a program branch:

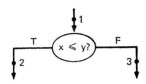

At point 2 our goal is already achieved. At point 3 we know that $\sim(x \leqslant y)$, i.e., $x > y$. To achieve $x \leqslant y$, it suffices to establish $x < y$, but this may be achieved by executing $interchange(x\ y)$. Thus we have $x \leqslant y$ in both worlds, and the final program is therefore:

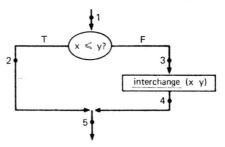

This example introduced no difficulties that our LISP-like program synthesis techniques could not handle. However, in general, programs with side effects must be given special treatment because of the necessity for representing changes in the world. It is important to be able to determine whether a given assertion is always true at a given point in a program. To this end we study the relationship between assertions and program constructs in the next section.

2.7. Assertions and Program Constructs

Suppose a program contains an assignment statement

and we wish to determine if $x \leqslant 3$ at Point 2. In order to do this it suffices to check if what we know at Point 1 implies that $y \leqslant 3$. In general, to determine an assertion of form $P(x)$ at Point 2, check $P(y)$ at Point 1. We will say that the assertion $P(y)$ is the result of "passing back" the assertion $P(x)$ from Point 2 to Point 1. [This is precisely the process outlined by Floyd (1967) and Hoare (1969).]
    Furthermore, if our program contains the instruction

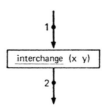

and we wish to establish $x \leqslant y$ at Point 2 we must check if $y \leqslant x$ at Point 1. In general, an assertion of form $P(x\ y)$ results in an assertion of form $P(y\ x)$ when passed back over *interchange*$(x\ y)$.

Suppose the program being constructed contains a branch

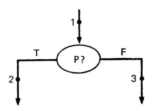

To determine if an assertion Q is true at Point 2, it suffices to check whether

$$Q \quad \text{if} \quad P$$

(i.e., $P \supset Q$) is true at Point 1. In order to determine if R is true at Point 3, it suffices to check whether

$$R \quad \text{if} \quad \sim P$$

(i.e., $\sim P \supset R$) is true at Point 1.

Suppose two control paths join in the program being constructed:

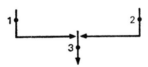

Thus to determine if assertion P is true at Point 3, it is sufficient to check that P be true at both Point 1 and Point 2.

Assertions may be passed back over complex programs. For instance, let us pass the assertion $y \leqslant z$ back over the program *sort*$(x\ y)$ which we constructed in the previous section. (See Figure 3.1.) By combining the methods that we have just introduced for passing assertions back over program constructs, we can see that in order to establish $y \leqslant z$ at Point 5, it is necessary to check that $(y \leqslant z$ if $x \leqslant y)$ and $(x \leqslant z$ if $\sim(x \leqslant y))$ are true at Point 1.

Often the specification of a program will require the simultaneous satisfaction of more than one goal. As in the case of conjunctive goals in LISP-like programs, the special interest of this problem lies in

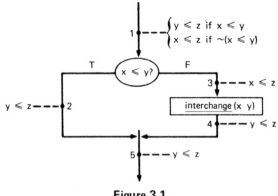

Figure 3.1.

the interrelatedness of the goals. The techniques of this section will now be applied to handle the interaction between goals.

2.8. Simultaneous Goals

A simultaneous-goal problem has the form

Achieve P and Q.

Sometimes P and Q will be independent conditions, so that we can achieve P and Q simply by achieving P and then achieving Q. For example, if our goal is

Achieve $x = 2$ and $y = 3$,

the two goals $x = 2$ and $y = 3$ are completely independent. In this section, however, we will be concerned with the more complex case in which P and Q interact. In such a case we may make P false in the course of achieving Q.

Consider for example the problem of sorting three variables x, y, and z. We will assume that the only instruction we can use is the subroutine $sort(u\ v)$, described in the previous section, which sorts two variables. Our goal is then

Achieve $x \leqslant y$ and $y \leqslant z$.

We know that the program $sort(u\ v)$ will achieve a goal of form $u \leqslant$

v. If we apply the straightforward technique of achieving the conjunct $x \leqslant y$ first, and then the conjunct $y \leqslant z$, we obtain the program

$$sort(x\ y)$$
$$sort(y\ z).$$

However, this program has a bug in that sorting y and z may disrupt the relation $x \leqslant y$: if z is initially the smallest of the three, in interchanging y and z we make y less than x. Reversing the order in which the conjuncts are achieved does not solve the problem.

There are a number of ways in which this problem may be resolved. One of them involves the notion of program modification [cf. Sussman (1975)]. The general strategy is as follows: to achieve P and Q simultaneously, first write a program to achieve P; then modify that program to achieve Q as well. The essence of this strategy, then, lies in a technique of program modification.

Let us see how this strategy applies to the simple sort problem. The specification is

Achieve $x \leqslant y$ and $y \leqslant z$.

It is easy to achieve $x \leqslant y$; the program $sort(x\ y)$ will do that immediately. We must now modify the program $sort(x\ y)$ to achieve $y \leqslant z$ without disturbing the relation $x \leqslant y$ we have just achieved. In other words, we would like to "protect" the relation $x \leqslant y$. We have seen that simply achieving $y \leqslant z$ after achieving $x \leqslant y$ is impossible without disturbing the protected relation. Therefore we will pass the goal $y \leqslant z$ back to the beginning of the program $sort(x\ y)$ and try to achieve it there, where there are no protected relations.

We have seen in the previous section that the goal $y \leqslant z$ passed back before the program $sort(x\ y)$ results in two goals:

(i) $y \leqslant z$ if $x \leqslant y$, and
(ii) $x \leqslant z$ if $\sim(x \leqslant y)$.

Both of these goals must be achieved before applying $sort(x\ y)$. We can achieve (i) by applying $sort(y\ z)$. (This will achieve $y \leqslant z$ whether or not $x \leqslant y$.) Our program so far is thus

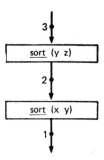

We still need to achieve goal (ii) at Point 2; we can achieve this goal simply by inserting the instruction $sort(x\ z)$ before Point 2.

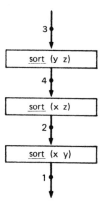

This modification will not effect Relation (i), "$y \leqslant z$ if $x \leqslant y$", which is protected at Point 2, because after executing $sort(y\ z)$ and $sort(x\ z)$, the value of z will be the largest of the three. Thus the desired program is

$$sort(y\ z)$$
$$sort(x\ z)$$
$$sort(x\ y).$$

If the subgoals are pursued in a different order, different variations on this program are obtained.

The program-modification strategy seems to be a fairly general approach to the simultaneous-goal problem. It also is a powerful program synthesis technique in general, as we will see when we develop the unification algorithm in Section 4.

This concludes the presentation of our basic program synthesis techniques. In the next part we will show how these same techniques work together in the synthesis of a more complex example.

3. Program Synthesis: The Pattern Matcher

We will present the synthesis of a simple pattern matcher to show how the concepts discussed in the previous section can be applied to a nontrivial problem. Later, in Section 4, we shall show how we can construct a more complex program, the unification algorithm of Robinson (1965), by modifying the pattern-matching program we are about to synthesize. We must first describe the data structures and primitive operations involved in the pattern matching and unification problems.

3.1. Domain and Notation

The main objects in our domain are *expressions* and *substitutions*.

3.1.1. Expressions

Expressions are atoms or nested lists of atoms; e.g., $(A\ B\ (X\ C)\ D)$ is an expression. An *atom* may be either a *variable* or a *constant*. (In our examples we will use $A, B, C, \ldots$ for constants and $U, V, W, \ldots$ for variables.) We have basic predicates *atom, var,* and *const* to distinguish these objects:

$$atom(l) \equiv l \text{ is an atom,}$$
$$var(l) \equiv l \text{ is a variable,}$$
$$const(l) \equiv l \text{ is a constant.}$$

To decompose an expression, we will use the primitive functions *head*(*l*) and *tail*(*l*), defined when *l* is not an atom.

head(*l*) is the first element of *l*.
tail(*l*) is the list of all but the first element of *l*.

Thus

$head(((A\ (X)\ B)\ C\ (D\ X))) = (A\ (X)\ B),$
$tail(((A\ (X)\ B)\ C\ (D\ X))) = (C\ (D\ X)).$

We will abbreviate $head(l)$ as l_h and $tail(l)$ as l_t.

To construct expressions we have the "$\cdot$" function: if l is any expression and m is a nonatomic expression, $l \cdot m$ is the expression formed by inserting l before the first element of m. For example,

$A \cdot (B\ C\ D) = (A\ B\ C\ D),$
$(A\ (X)\ B) \cdot (C\ (D\ X)) = ((A\ (X)\ B)\ C\ (D\ X)).$

The predicate $occursin(x\ l)$ is true if x is an atom that occurs in expression l at any level, e.g.,

$occursin(A\ (C\ (B\ (A)\ B)\ C))$ is true,

but

$occursin(X\ Y)$ is false.

Finally, we will introduce the predicate $constexp(l)$, which is true if l is made up entirely of constants. Thus

$constexp((A\ (B)\ C\ (D\ E)))$ is true.

but

$constexp(X)$ is false.

Note that $constexp$ differs from $const$ in that $constexp$ may be true for nonatomic expressions.

3.1.2. Substitutions

A substitution replaces certain variables of an expression by other expressions. We will represent a substitution as a list of pairs. Thus

$(\langle X\ (A\ B)\rangle\ \langle Y\ (C\ Y)\rangle)$

is a substitution.

The instantiation function $inst(s\ l)$ applies the substitution s to the expression l. For example, if

$s = (\langle X\ (A\ B)\rangle\ \langle Y\ (C\ Y)\rangle)$ and $l = (X\ (A\ Y)\ X),$

then

$inst(s\ l) = ((A\ B)\ (A\ (C\ Y))\ (A\ B)).$

Note that the substitution is applied by first replacing all occurrences of X simultaneously by $(A\ B)$ and then all occurrences of Y simultaneously by $(C\ Y)$. Thus, if

$$s' = (\langle X\ Y\rangle\ \langle Y\ C\rangle),$$

then

$$inst(s'\ l) = (C\ (A\ C)\ C).$$

The empty substitution Λ is represented by the empty list of pairs. Thus for any expression l,

$$inst(\Lambda\ l) = l.$$

We regard two substitutions s_1 and s_2 as equal (written $s_1 = s_2$) if and only if

$$inst(s_1\ l) = inst(s_2\ l)$$

for every expression l. Thus

$$(\langle X\ Y\rangle\ \langle Y\ C\rangle) \quad \text{and} \quad (\langle X\ C\rangle\ \langle Y\ C\rangle)$$

are regarded as equal substitutions.

We can build up substitutions by using the functions *pair* and $\circ$ (composition): If v is a variable and t an expression, $pair(v\ t)$ is the substitution that replaces v by t; i.e.,

$$pair\,(v\ t) = (\langle v\ t\rangle).$$

If s_1 and s_2 are two substitutions, $s_1 \circ s_2$ is the substitution with the same effect as applying s_1 followed by s_2. Thus

$$inst(s_1 \circ s_2\ l) = inst(s_2\ \ inst(s_1\ l)).$$

For example if

$$s_1 = (\langle X\ A\rangle\ \langle Y\ B\ \rangle) \quad \text{and} \quad s_2 = (\langle Z\ C\rangle\ \langle X\ D\rangle),$$

then

$$s_1 \circ s_2 = (\langle X\ A\rangle\ \langle Y\ B\rangle\ \langle Z\ C\rangle).$$

Note that for the empty substitution Λ,

$$\Lambda \circ s = s \circ \Lambda = s$$

for any substitution s.

3.2. The Specifications

The problem of pattern matching may be described as follows. We are given two expressions, *pat* and *arg*. While *pat* can be any expression, *arg* is assumed to contain no variables; i.e., *constexp*(*arg*) is true. We want to find a substitution z that transforms *pat* into *arg*, i.e., such that

$$inst(z\ pat) = arg.$$

We will call such a substitution a *match*. If no match exists, we want the program to return the distinguished constant NOMATCH. For example, if

$$pat \text{ is } (X\ A\ (Y\ B)) \text{ and } arg \text{ is } (C\ A\ (D\ B)),$$

we want the program to find the match

$$(\langle X\ C\rangle\ \langle Y\ D\rangle).$$

On the other hand, if

$$pat \text{ is } (X\ A\ (X\ B)) \text{ and } arg \text{ is } (B\ A\ (D\ B)),$$

then no substitution will transform *pat* into *arg*, because X cannot be matched with both B and D. Therefore the program should yield NOMATCH. (This version of the pattern matcher is simpler than the pattern matching algorithms usually implemented in programming languages because of the absence of "sequence" or "fragment" variables. Our variables must match exactly one expression, whereas a fragment variable may match any number of expressions.)

In mathematical notation the specifications for our pattern matcher are:

Goal 1. *match*(*pat arg*) = Find z such that *inst*(*z pat*) = *arg*
                          else z = NOMATCH,

where "Find z such that $P(z)$ else $Q(z)$" means construct an output z satisfying $P(z)$ if one exists; otherwise, find a z such that $Q(z)$.

The above specifications do not completely capture our intentions; for instance, if

$$pat \text{ is } (X\ Y) \text{ and } arg \text{ is } (A\ B),$$

then the substitution

$$z = (\langle X\ A\rangle\ \langle Y\ B\rangle\ \langle Z\ C\rangle)$$

will satisfy our specifications as well as

$$z = (\langle X\ A\rangle\ \langle Y\ B\rangle).$$

We have neglected to include in our specifications that no substitutions should be made for variables that do not occur in *pat*. We will call a match that satisfies this additional condition a *most general match*.

An interesting characteristic of the synthesis we present is that even if the user does not require that the match found be most general, the system will strengthen the specifications automatically to imply this condition, using the method outlined in Section 2.4. Therefore we will begin the synthesis using the weaker specifications.

3.3. The Base Cases

Rather than list all the knowledge we require in a special section at the beginning, we will mention a rule only when it is about to be used. Furthermore, if a rule seems excessively trivial we will omit it entirely. The general strategy is to first work on

Goal 2. Find z such that $inst(z\ pat) = arg$.

If this is found to be impossible (i.e., if it is *proven* that no such z exists), we will work on

Goal 3. Find a z such that z = NOMATCH;

which is seen to be trivially satisfied by taking z to be NOMATCH.

Thus, from now on we will be working primarily on Goal 2. However, in working on any goal we devote a portion of our time to showing that the goal is impossible to achieve. When we find cases in which Goal 2 is proven impossible, we will automatically return NOMATCH, which satisfies Goal 3.

We have in our knowledge base a number of rules concerning *inst,* including

Rule 1. $inst(s\ \ x) = x$ for any substitution s if $constexp(x)$
Rule 2. $inst(pair(v\ t)\ \ v) = t$ if $var(v)$.

We assume that these rules are retrieved by pattern-directed function invocation on Goal 2. Rule 1 can be applied only in the case that $constexp(pat)$ and $pat = arg$. We cannot prove either of these conditions; their truth or falsehood depends on the particular inputs to the program. We use these predicates as conditions for a hypothetical world split. In the case that both of these conditions are true, Rule 1 tells us that *any* substitution is a satisfactory match. We will have occasion to tighten the specifications of our program later; as they stand now, we will simply return "any", so as not to restrict our choice. The portion of the program we have constructed so far reads

$$match(pat\ arg) =$$
$$\text{if } constexp(pat)$$
$$\text{then if } pat = arg$$
$$\text{then any}$$
$$\text{else } \dots \ .$$

On the other hand, in the case $constexp(pat)$ and $pat \neq arg$, Rule 1 tells us that

$$inst(z\ pat) = pat \neq arg$$

for any z. Hence we are led to satisfy Goal 3 by returning NOMATCH.
    We now consider the case

$$\sim constexp(pat).$$

Rule 2 establishes the subgoal

$$var(pat).$$

This is another occasion for a hypothetical world split. When $var(pat)$ is true, the program must return $pair(pat\ arg)$; the program we have constructed so far is

$$match(pat\ arg) =$$
$$\text{if } constexp(pat)$$
$$\text{then if } pat = arg$$
$$\text{then any}$$
$$\text{else NOMATCH}$$
$$\text{else if } var(pat)$$
$$\text{then } pair(pat\ arg)$$
$$\text{else } \dots \ .$$

Hencefore we assume $\sim var(pat)$. Recall that we have been assuming also that $\sim constexp(pat)$. To proceed we make use of the following additional knowledge about the function *inst*:

Rule 3. $inst(s \quad x \cdot y) \;=\; inst(s \quad x) \cdot inst(s \quad y)$
          for any substitution *s*.

This rule applies to our Goal 2 if $pat = x \cdot y$ for some expressions *x* and *y*. We have some additional knowledge about expressions in general:

Rule 4. $u \;=\; u_h \cdot u_t$ if $\sim atom(u)$.

Recall that u_h is an abbreviation for *head(u)* and u_t is an abbreviation for *tail(u)*.

Rule 5. $u \neq v \cdot w$ for any *v* and *w* if *atom(u)*.

Using Rule 4, we generate a subgoal

$$\sim atom(pat).$$

Since we have already assumed $\sim constexp(pat)$ and $\sim var(pat)$, we can actually prove $\sim atom(pat)$ using knowledge in the system. Therefore $pat = pat_h \cdot pat_t$, and using Rule 3 our Goal 2 is then reduced to

Goal 4. Find *z* such that $inst(z \; pat_h) \cdot inst(z \; pat_t) = \text{arg}$.

We now make use of some general list-processing knowledge.

Rule 6. To prove $x \cdot y = u \cdot v$,   prove $x = u$ and $y = v$.

Applying this rule, we generate a subgoal to show that

$$arg = u \cdot v$$

for some *u* and *v*. Applying Rule 4, we know this is true with $u = arg_h$ and $v = arg_t$ if

$$\sim atom(arg).$$

This is another occasion for a hypothetical world split.

Thus, by Rule 6, in the case that $\sim atom(arg)$, our subgoal reduces to

Goal 5. Find z such that

$$inst(z\ pat_h) = arg_h$$

and

$$inst(z\ pat_t) = arg_t.$$

We will postpone treatment of this goal until after we have considered the other case, in which

$$atom(arg)$$

holds. In this case Rule 5 tells us that

$$inst(z\ pat_h) \cdot inst(z\ pat_t) \neq arg$$

for any z. Hence, our goal is unachievable in this case, and we can return NOMATCH.

The program so far is

```
match(pat arg) =
  if constexp(pat)
  then if pat = arg
       then any
       else NOMATCH
  else if var(pat)
       then pair(pat arg)
       else if atom(arg)
            then NOMATCH
            else... .
```

For the as yet untreated case neither *pat* nor *arg* is atomic. Henceforth using Rule 4 we assume that *pat* is $pat_h \cdot pat_t$ and *arg* is $arg_h \cdot arg_t$.

3.4. The Inductive Case

We will describe the remainder of the synthesis in less detail, because the reader has already seen the style of reasoning we have been using. Recall that we had postponed our discussion of Goal 5 in order to consider the case in which *arg* is atomic. Now that we have completed our development of that case, we resume our work on Goal 5:

Find z such that $inst(z \; pat_h) = arg_h$ and $inst(z \; pat_t) = arg_t$.

This is a conjunctive goal, and is treated analogously to the goal in the simultaneous-linear-equations example (Section 2.5): The system will attempt to solve the first conjunct, using a recursive call to the pattern-matcher itself.

The interaction between the two conjuncts is part of the challenge of this synthesis. It is quite possible to satisfy each conjunct separately without being able to satisfy them both together. For example, if $pat = (X \; X)$ and $arg = (A \; B)$, then $pat_h = X$, $pat_t = (X)$, $arg_h = A$, and $arg_t = (B)$. Thus $z = (\langle X \; A \rangle)$ satisfies the first conjunct, $z = (\langle X \; B \rangle)$ satisfies the second conjunct, but no substitution will satisfy both conjuncts, because no substitution can match X against both A and B. Some mechanism is needed to ensure that the expression assigned to a variable in solving the first conjunct is the same as the expression assigned to that variable in solving the second conjunct.

There are several ways to approach this difficulty. For instance, the programmer may satisfy the two conjuncts separately and then attempt to combine the two substitutions thereby derived into a single substitution. Or he may actually replace those variables in pat_t that also occur in pat_h by whatever expressions they have been matched against, before attempting to match pat_t against arg_t. Or he may simply pass the substitution that satisfied the first conjunct as a third argument to the pattern matcher in working on the second conjunct. The pattern matcher must then check that the matches assigned to variables are consistent with the substitution given as the third argument.

We will examine in this section how a system would discover the second of these methods. A similar system could also discover the third method. We will not consider the first method here because it is not easily adapted to the unification problem.

Our strategy for approaching the conjunctive goal is as follows. We will consider the first conjunct independently:

Goal 6. Find z such that $inst(z \; pat_h) = arg_h$.

If we find a z that satisfies this goal, we will substitute that z into the second conjunct, giving

Goal 7. Prove $inst(z\ pat_t) = arg_t$.

If we are successful in Goal 7, we are done; however, if we fail, we will try to generalize z. In other words, we will try to find a broader class of substitutions that satisfy Goal 6 and from these select one that also satisfies Goal 7. This is the method we introduced to solve conjunctive goals in Section 2.5.

Applying this strategy, we begin work on Goal 6. We first use a rule that relates the construct

Find z such that $P(z)$

to the construct

Find z such that $P(z)$ else $Q(z)$.

Rule 7. To find z such that $P(z)$, it suffices to find z_1 such that $P(z_1)$ else $Q(z_1)$), and $\sim Q(z_1)$ for some predicate Q.

This rule, applied to Goal 6, causes the generation of the subgoal

Goal 8. Find z_1 such that $inst(z_1\ pat_h) = arg_h$ else $Q(z_1)$, and $\sim Q(z_1)$.

The first conjunct of this subgoal matches the top-level Goal 1, where $Q(z_1)$ is z_1 = NOMATCH. This suggests establishing a recursion at this point, taking

$$z_1 = match(pat_h\ arg_h).$$

Henceforth we will use z_1 as an abbreviation for $match(pat_h\ arg_h)$. Termination is easily shown, because both pat_h and arg_h are proper subexpressions of pat and arg, respectively. It remains to show, according to Rule 7, that $z_1 \neq$ NOMATCH. This causes another hypothetical world split: in the case z_1 = NOMATCH (i.e., no substitution can cause pat_h and arg_h to match), we can show that no substitution can cause pat and arg to match either, and hence can take z = NOMATCH.

We have thus constructed the following new program segment

$$z_1 \leftarrow match(pat_h \ arg_h)$$
$$\text{if } z_1 = \text{NOMATCH}$$
$$\text{then NOMATCH}$$
$$\text{else. . .}$$

We have used z_1 as a program variable to improve readability. The actual program constructed would use $match(pat_h \ arg_h)$ itself in place of z_1.

On the other hand, if $z_1 \neq$ NOMATCH, we know that z_1 satisfies the first conjunct (Goal 6). Thus, in keeping with the conjunctive goal strategy, we try to show that z_1 satisfies the second conjunct (Goal 7) as well, i.e.,

$$inst(z_1 \ pat_t) = arg_t.$$

However, we fail in this attempt; in fact we can find sample inputs *pat* and *arg* that provide a counterexample to Goal 7 [e.g., *pat* = $(A \ X)$, *arg* = $(A \ B)$, $z_1 = \Lambda$]. Thus we go back and try to generalize our solution to Goal 6.

We already have a solution to Goal 6: we know $inst(z_1 \ pat_h) = arg_h$. We also can deduce that $constexp(arg_h)$, because we have assumed $constexp(arg)$. Hence Rule 1 tells us that

$$inst(z_2 \ arg_h) = arg_h$$

for any substitution z_2. Therefore

$$inst(z_2 \ inst(z_1 \ pat_h)) = arg_h,$$

i.e.,

$$inst(z_1 \circ z_2 \ pat_h) = arg_h$$

for any substitution z_2. Thus having one substitution z_1 that satisfies Goal 6, we have an entire class of substitutions, of form $z_1 \circ z_2$, each of which satisfies Goal 6. These substitutions may be considered to be "extensions" of z_1; although z_1 itself may not satisfy Goal 7, perhaps some extension of z_1 will.

The above reasoning is straightforward enough to justify, but further work is needed to motivate a machine to pursue it.

It remains now to find a single z_2 such that $z_1 \circ z_2$ satisfies Goal

7, i.e.,

Goal 9. Find z_1 such that $inst(z_1 \circ z_2 \ pat_t) = arg_t$, or equivalently,
    Find z_2 such that $inst(z_2 \ inst(z_1 \ pat_t)) = arg_t$.
Applying Rule 7, we establish a new goal:

Goal 10. Find z_2 such that $inst(z_2 \ inst(z_1 \ pat_t)) = arg_t$ else $Q(z_2)$,
    and $\sim Q(z_2)$.

The first conjunct of this goal is an instance of our top-level goal,
taking *pat* to be $inst(z_1 \ pat_t)$, *arg* to be arg_t, and $Q(z_2)$ to be $z_2 =$
NOMATCH. Thus we attempt to insert the recursive call

$$z_2 \leftarrow match(inst(z_1 \ pat_t) \ arg_t)$$

into our program at this point. (Again, the introduction of z_2 as a
program variable is for notational simplicity.) However, we must
first establish

$$\sim Q(z_2),$$

i.e.,

$$z_2 \neq \text{NOMATCH}.$$

We cannot prove this: it is true for some examples and false for
others. Therefore we split on this condition.

In the case $z_2 \neq$ NOMATCH Goal 10 is satisfied. Thus z_2 also
satisfies Goal 9, and $z = z_1 \circ z_2$ satisfies Goal 7.

Our program so far is

```
match(pat arg) =
  if constexp(pat)
  then if pat = arg
       then any
       else NOMATCH
  else if var(pat)
       then pair(pat arg)
       else if atom(arg)
            then NOMATCH
            else z₁ ← match(patₕ argₕ)
                 if z₁ = NOMATCH
```

then NOMATCH

else $z_2 \leftarrow match(inst(z_1\ pat_t)\ arg_t)$

if z_2 = NOMATCH

then. . .

else $z_1 \circ z_2$.

3.5. The Strengthening of the Specifications

We have gone this far through the synthesis using the weak specifications, i.e., without requiring that the match found be most general. In fact, the match found may or may not be most general, depending on the value taken for the unspecified substitution "any" produced in the very first case. The synthesis is nearly complete. However, we will be unable to continue it without strengthening the specifications and modifying the program accordingly. We now have only one case left to consider. This is the case in which

$$z_2 = \text{NOMATCH},$$

i.e.,

$$match(inst(z_1\ pat_t)\ arg_t) = \text{NOMATCH}.$$

This means that no substitution w satisfies

$$inst(w\ \ inst(z_1\ pat_t)) = arg_t,$$

or, equivalently,

$$inst(z_1 \circ w\ \ pat_t) \neq arg_t \quad \text{for every substitution } w.$$

This means that no substitution of form $z_1 \circ w$ could possibly satisfy

$$inst(z_1 \circ w\ \ pat) = arg.$$

We here have a choice: we can try to find a substitution s not of form $z_1 \circ w$ that satisfies.

$$inst(s\ pat_h) = arg_h$$

and repeat the process; or we could try to show that only a substitution s of form $z_1 \circ w$ could possibly satisfy

$$inst(s\ pat_h) = arg_h,$$

and therefore we take z = NOMATCH.

Pursuing the latter course, we try to show that the set of substitutions s of form $z_1 \circ w$ is the entire set of solutions to

$$inst(s\ pat_h) = arg_h.$$

In other words, we show that for any substitution s,

$$\text{if } inst(s\ pat_h) = arg_h \quad \text{then } s = z_1 \circ w \text{ for some } w.$$

This condition is equivalent to saying that z_1 is a most general match. We cannot prove this about z_1 itself; however, since z_1 is $match(pat_h\ arg_h)$, it suffices to add the condition to the specifications for $match$, as described in Section 2.4. The strengthened specifications now read

> Find z such that
> $\{inst(z\ pat) = arg$ and
> for all s [if $inst(s\ pat) = arg$
>   then $s = z \circ w$ for some w]$\}$
> else $z = $ NOMATCH.

Once we have strengthened the specifications it is necessary to go through the entire program and see that the new, stronger specifications are satisfied, modifying the program if necessary. In this case no major modifications are necessary; however, the assignment

$$z \leftarrow \text{any}$$

that occurs in the case in which pat and arg are equal and constant is further specified to read

$$z \leftarrow \Lambda.$$

Our final program is therefore

$$match(pat\ arg) =$$
$$\text{if } constexp(pat)$$
$$\text{then if } pat = arg$$
$$\quad\text{then } \Lambda$$
$$\quad\text{else NOMATCH}$$
$$\text{else if } var(pat)$$
$$\quad\text{then } pair(pat\ arg)$$
$$\quad\text{else if } atom(arg)$$
$$\quad\quad\text{then NOMATCH}$$
$$\quad\quad\text{else } z_1 \leftarrow match(pat_h\ arg_h)$$
$$\quad\quad\quad\text{if } z_1 = \text{NOMATCH}$$

$$\text{then NOMATCH}$$
$$\text{else } z_2 \leftarrow match(inst(z_1 \ pat_t) \ arg_t)$$
$$\text{if } z_2 = \text{NOMATCH}$$
$$\text{then NOMATCH}$$
$$\text{else } z_1 \circ z_2.$$

The above pattern matcher is only one of many pattern-matchers that can be derived to satisfy the same specifications. In pursuing the synthesis the system has made many choices; some of the alternative paths result in a failure to solve the problem altogether, whereas other paths result in different, possibly better programs.

4. Program Modification: The Unification Algorithm

In general, we cannot expect a system to synthesize an entire complex program from scratch, as in the pattern-matcher example. We would like the system to remember a large body of programs that have been synthesized before, and the method by which they were constructed. When presented with a new problem, the system should check to see if it has solved a similar problem before. If so, it may be able to adapt the technique of the old program to make it solve the new problem.

There are several difficulties involved in this approach. First, we cannot expect the system to remember every detail of every synthesis in its history. Therefore, it must decide what to remember and what to forget. Second, the system must decide which problems are similar to the one being considered, and the concept of similarity is somewhat ill defined. Third, having found a similar program, the system must somehow modify the old synthesis to solve the new problem. We will concentrate only on the last of these problems in this discussion. We will illustrate a technique for program modification as applied to the synthesis of a version of Robinson's unification algorithm (1965).

4.1. The Specifications

Unification may be considered to be a generalization of pattern-matching in which variables appear in both *pat* and *arg*. The problem is to find a single substitution (called a "unifier") that, when applied to both *pat* and *arg*, will yield identical expressions. For instance, if

$$pat = (X\ A)$$

and

$$arg = (B\ Y),$$

then a possible unifier of *pat* and *arg* is

$$(\langle X\ B\rangle\ \langle Y\ A\rangle).$$

The close analogy between pattern-matching and unification is clear. If we assume that the system remembers the pattern-matcher we constructed in Sections 3.2 through 3.5 and the goal structure involved in the synthesis, the solution to the unification problem is greatly facilitated.

The specifications for the unification algorithm, in mathematical notation, are

> $unify(pat\ arg) =$
> Find z such that $inst(z\ pat) = inst(z\ arg)$
> else $z = $ NOUNIFY.

4.2. The Analogy with the Pattern Matcher

For purpose of comparison we rewrite the *match* specifications:

> $match(pat\ arg) =$
> Find z such that $inst(z\ pat) = arg$
> else $z = $ NOMATCH.

In formulating the analogy, we identify *unify* with *match*, *pat* with *pat*, the *arg* in *unify(pat arg)* with *arg*, *inst(z arg)* also with *arg*, and NOMATCH with NOUNIFY. In accordance with this analogy, we must systematically alter the goal structure of the pattern-matcher synthesis. For example, Goal 5 becomes modified to read

> Find z such that $inst(z\ pat_h) = inst(z\ arg_h)$
> and $inst(z\ pat_t) = inst\ (z\ arg_t)$.

In constructing the pattern matcher, we had to break down the synthesis into various cases. We will try to maintain this case structure in formulating our new program. Much of the saving derived from modifying the pattern matcher instead of constructing the unification algorithm from scratch arises because we do not have to deduce the case splitting all over again.

A difficult step in the pattern matcher synthesis involved the strengthening of the specifications for the entire program. We added the condition that the match found was to be "most general". In formulating the unification synthesis, we will immediately strengthen the specifications in the analogous way. The strengthened specifications read

$$unify(pat\ arg) =$$
Find z such that
$$\{\ inst(z\ pat) = inst(z\ arg)\ \text{and}$$
$$\text{for all } s\ [\text{if } inst(s\ pat) = inst(s\ arg)$$
$$\text{then } s = z \circ w \text{ for some } w\ ]\}$$
else $z = $ NOUNIFY.

Following Robinson, we will refer to a unifier satisfying the new condition as a "most general unifier".

Note that this alteration process is purely syntactic; there is no reason to assume that the altered goal structure corresponds to a valid line of reasoning. For instance, the mere fact that achieving Goal 2 in the pattern-matching program is useful in achieving Goal 1 does not necessarily imply that achieving the corresponding Goal 2′ in the unification algorithm will have any bearing on Goal 1′. The extent to which the reasoning carries over depends on the soundness of the analogy. If a portion of the altered goal structure proves to be valid, the corresponding segment of the program can remain; otherwise, we must construct a new program segment.

4.3. The Modification

Let us examine the first two cases of the unification synthesis in full detail, so that we can see exactly how the modification process works. In the pattern matcher, we generated the subgoal (Goal 2)

$$\text{Find } z \text{ such that } inst(z\ pat) = arg.$$

The corresponding unification subgoal is

$$\text{Find } z \text{ such that } inst(z\ pat) = inst(z\ arg).$$

In the pattern matcher we first considered the case $constexp(pat)$ where $pat = arg$. In this case the corresponding program segment will return Λ. This segment also satisfies the modified goal in this case, because

$$inst(\Lambda\ pat) = inst(\Lambda\ arg).$$

The system must also check that Λ is a most general unifier, i.e.,

for all s [if $inst(s\ pat) = inst(s\ arg)$

then $s = \Lambda \circ w$ for some w].

This condition is easily satisfied, taking $w = s$. Thus, in this case, the program segment is correct without any modification.

The next case does require some modification. In the pattern matcher, when $constexp(pat)$ is true and $pat \neq arg$, z is taken to be NOMATCH. However, in this case in the unification algorithm we must check that

$$inst(s\ pat) \neq inst(s\ arg),$$
i.e.,

$$pat \neq inst(s\ arg)$$

for any s, in order to take $z =$ NOUNIFY. Since for the unification problem arg may contain variables, this condition cannot be satisfied. We must therefore try to achieve the specifications in some other way. In this case [where $constexp(pat)$], the specifications of the unification algorithm reduce to

Find z such that
$\{pat = inst(z\ arg)$ and
for all s [if $pat = inst(s\ arg)$
then $s = z \circ w$ for some w]$\}$
else $z =$ NOUNIFY.

These specifications are precisely the specifications of the pattern matcher with pat and arg reversed; consequently, we can invoke $match(arg\ pat)$ at this point in the program.

The balance of the modification can be carried out in the same manner. The derived unification algorithm is

$unify(pat\ arg) =$
  if $constexp(pat)$
  then if $pat = arg$
      then Λ
      else $match(arg\ pat)$

    else if $var(pat)$
       then if $occursin(pat\ arg)$
       then NOUNIFY
       else $pair(pat\ arg)$
    else if $atom(arg)$
       then $unify(arg\ pat)$
       else $z_1 \leftarrow unify(pat_h\ arg_h)$
         if z_1 = NOUNIFY
         then NOUNIFY
         else $z_2 \leftarrow unify(inst(z_1\ pat_t)\ \ inst(z_1\ arg_t))$
           if z_2 = NOUNIFY
           then NOUNIFY
           else $z_1 \circ z_2$.

Recall that $occursin(pat\ arg)$ means that pat occurs in arg as a sub-expression.

The termination of this program is considerably more difficult to prove than was the termination of the pattern matcher. However, the construction of the unification algorithm from the pattern matcher is much easier than the initial synthesis of the pattern matcher itself.

Note that the program we have constructed contains a redundant branch. The expression

    if $pat = arg$
    then Λ
    else $match(arg\ pat)$

could be reduced to

$$match(arg\ pat).$$

Such improvements would not be made until a later optimization phase.

5. Discussion

5.1. Implementation

Implementation of the techniques presented in this paper is underway. Some of them have already been implemented. Others will require further development before an implementation will be possible.

We imagine the rules, used to represent reasoning tactics, to be expressed as programs in a PLANNER -type language. Our own implementation is in QLISP (Wilber, 1976). Rules are summoned by pattern-directed function invocation.

World splitting has been implemented using the *context* mechanism of QLISP, which was introduced in QA4 [Rulifson et al., (1972)]. Although the world splitting has been implemented, we have yet to experiment with the various strategies for controlling it.

The existing system is capable of producing simple programs such as the union function, the program to sort two variables from Section 2, or the loop-free segments of the pattern-matcher from Section 3.

The generalization of specifications (Section 2.4 and 3.5) is a difficult technique to apply without its going astray. We will develop heuristics to regulate it in the course of the implementation. Similarly, our approach to conjunctive goals (Section 2.5) needs further explication.

5.2. Historical Context and Contemporary Research

Early work in program synthesis [e.g., Simon (1963), Green (1969), Waldinger and Lee (1969)] was limited by the problem-solving capabilities of the respective formalisms involved (the General Problem Solver in the case of Simon; resolution-theorem-proving in the case of the others). Our paper on loop formation (Manna and Waldinger, 1971) was set in a theorem-proving framework, and paid little attention to the implementation problems.

It is typical of contemporary program synthesis work not to attempt to restrict itself to a formalism; systems are more likely to write programs the way a human programmer would write them. For example, the recent work of Sussman (1975) is modeled after the debugging process. Rather than trying to produce a correct program at once, Sussman's system rashly goes ahead and writes incorrect programs which it then proceeds to debug. The work reported in Green (1976) attempts to model a very experienced programmer. The system relies on built-in knowledge rather than on inference or problem solving ability.

The work reported here emphasizes reasoning more heavily than the papers of Sussman and Green. For instance, in our synthesis of the pattern matcher we assumed no knowledge about pattern matching itself. Of course we do assume extensive knowledge of lists, substitutions, and other aspects of the subject domain.

Although Sussman's debugging approach has influenced our treatment of program modification and the handling of simultaneous goals, we tend to rely more on logical methods than Sussman. Furthermore, Sussman deals only with programs that manipulate blocks on a table; therefore he has not been forced to deal with problems that are more crucial in conventional programming, such as the formation of conditionals and loops.

The work of Buchanan and Luckham (1974) is closest to ours in the problems it addresses. However, their system forms iterative loops that must be specified in advance by the user as "iterative rules", whereas in our system the loops are recursive and are introduced by the system itself when it recognizes a relationship between the top-level goal and a subgoal. Buchanan and Luckham's methods for forming conditionals and for treating programs with side effects are also somewhat different from ours.

5.3. Conclusion and Future Work

Some of the approaches to program synthesis that we feel will be most fruitful in the future have been given little emphasis in this paper because they are not yet fully developed. For example, the technique of program modification, which occupied only one small part of the current paper, we feel to be central to future program synthesis work. The retention of previously constructed programs is a powerful way to acquire and store knowledge. Furthermore, program optimization [cf. Darlington and Burstall (1973)] and program debugging are just special cases of program modification.

We hope we have managed to convey in this paper the promise of program synthesis, without giving the false impression that automatic synthesis is likely to be immediately practical. A computer system that can replace the human programmer will very likely have human intelligence in other respects as well.

Acknowledgments

We wish to thank Robert Boyer, Nachum Dershowitz, Bertram Raphael, and Georgia Sutherland for detailed critical readings of the manuscript. We would also like to thank Peter Deutsch, Richard Fikes, Akira Fusaoka, Cordell Green and his students, Irene Greif, Carl Hewitt, Shmuel Katz, David Luckham, Earl Sacerdoti, and Ben Wegbreit for conversations that aided in formulating the ideas in this paper. The set-theoretic expression-handler is based on work of Jan Derksen.

The research reported herein was sponsored by the National Science Foundation primarily under Grant GJ-36146 (SRI Project 2245) and partially under Grant GK-35493 (SRI Project 2323).

Postscript

Since the original appearance of the papers in this collection, much related research has been done. In this postscript we do not catalogue all the papers that have appeared on these topics, but we do mention some closely related work and some general trends.

Program Verification

Since the paper "Reasoning about Programs" was written, several more powerful verification systems have appeared using the same invariant-assertion technique. The system of Suzuki (1975), for example, can handle a wider class of programs and is significantly faster than the system we describe. Good et al. (1975), on the other hand, allow much more interaction between the user and the theorem prover. Much work has been done also in extending the technique to allow a wider class of data and control structures in the verified programs. At the same time, alternate techniques for program verification besides the invariant-assertion method have been proposed.

Analysis of Programs

Much work has also been done related to the topic of the second paper, "Logical Analysis of Programs." German and Wegbreit (1975) have implemented some heuristic approaches for generating invariant assertions. The counters approach to proving program termination has been incorporated into the program verification system of Luckham and Suzuki (1975). A system to analyze the running time of programs has been implemented by Wegbreit (1975). Efforts have been made to use such analyses as a basis for the optimization of programs and as a guide for their synthesis.

179

Program Synthesis

The recursion-introduction technique that appears in "Knowledge and Reasoning in Program Synthesis" has been further developed by Siklóssy (1974) and Darlington (1975). The simultaneous goal strategy has been elaborated on and implemented by Warren (1974) and Waldinger (1977). Other approaches to the automatic construction of computer programs are being pursued, under the general rubric of *automatic programming.* Most of these approaches are less formal than ours in specifying the program to be constructed, and less systematic in developing it. For a comprehensive survey of this field, see Biermann (1976).

References

Balzer, R. M. (Sept. 1972). *Automatic Programming.* Technical Report. Information Science Institute, University of Southern California, Marina del Rey, Ca.

Biermann, A. W. (1976). Approaches to automatic programming. In *Advances in Computers,* vol. 15. New York: Academic Press (to appear).

Biermann, A. W. and R. Krishnaswamy (Sept. 1976). Constructing programs from example computations. *IEEE Transactions on Software Engineering,* 2 (3): 141–153.

Boyer, R. S., and J S. Moore (Jan. 1975). Proving theorems about LISP functions. *JACM,* 22(1): 129–144.

Buchanan, J. R., and D. C. Luckham (May 1974). *On Automating the Construction of Programs.* Technical report. Artificial Intelligence Laboratory, Stanford University, Stanford, Ca..

Burstall, R. M., and J. Darlington (Jan. 1977). A transformation system for developing recursive programs, *JACM,* 24 (1): 44–67.

Cooper, D. C. (1971). Programs for mechanical program verification. In *Machine Intelligence* 6, New York: Elsevier North-Holland, pp. 43–59.

Darlington, J. (July 1975). Applications of program transformation to program synthesis. In *Colloques IRIA on Proving and Improving Programs.* Arc et Senans, France, pp. 133–144.

Darlington, J., and R. M. Burstall (Aug. 1973). A system which automatically improves programs. *In Proceedings of the Third International Joint Conference on Artificial Intelligence,* Stanford, Ca., pp. 479–485.

Deutsch, L. P. (June 1973). *An Interactive Program Verifier.* Ph.D. thesis. University of California, Berkeley, Ca.

Elspas, B., K. N. Levitt, and R. J. Waldinger (Sept. 1973). *An Interactive System for the Verification of Computer Programs.* Technical report. Stanford Research Institute, Menlo Park, Ca..

Elspas, B. (July 1974). *The Semiautomatic Generation of Inductive Assertions for Proving Program Correctness*. Technical report. Stanford Research Institute, Menlo Park, Ca.

Floyd, R. W. (1967). Assigning meanings to programs. In *Proceedings of the Symposium in Applied Mathematics,* vol. 19 (J. T. Schwartz, ed.), American Mathematical Society, Providence, R. I., pp. 19-32.

Floyd, R. W. (1971). Towards interactive design of correct programs. In *Proceedings of IFIP Congress,* vol. 1, Amsterdam: North-Holland, pp. 7-10.

German, S. M., and B. Wegbreit (Mar. 1975). Proving loop programs. *IEEE Transactions on Software Engineering,* 1 (1): 68-75.

Good, D. I., R. L. London, and W. W. Bledsoe (Mar. 1975). An interactive program verification system. *IEEE Transactions on Software Engineering,* 1 (1): 59-67.

Green, C. (May 1969). Application of theorem proving to problem solving, In *Proceedings of International Joint Conference on Artificial Intelligence,* Washington, D.C. pp. 219-239.

Green, C. (Oct. 1976). The design of PSI program synthesis system. In *Proceedings of Second International Conference on Software Engineering.* San Francisco, Ca., pp. 4-18.

Greif, I. and R. Waldinger (April 1974). A more mechanical heuristic approach to program verification. In *Proceedings of International Symposium on Programming,* Paris, pp. 83-90.

Hardy, S. (Sept. 1975). Synthesis of LISP programs from examples, In *Proceedings of the Fourth International Joint Conference on Artificial Intelligence,* Tbilisi, Georgia, USSR, pp. 240-245.

Hewitt, C. (April 1971). *Description and Theoretical Analysis (Using Schemata) of PLANNER: A Language for Proving Theorems and Manipulating Models in a Robot.* Ph.D. thesis M.I.T., Cambridge, Mass.

Hoare, C. A. R. (July 1961). Algorithm 65: FIND, *CACM,* 4 (7): 321.

Hoare, C. A. R. (Oct. 1969). An axiomatic basis of computer programming, *CACM,* 12 (10): 576-580, 583.

Hoare, C. A. R. (Jan. 1971). Proof of a program: FIND. *CACM,* 14 (1): 39-45.

Igarashi, S., R. L. London, and D. C. Luckham (1975). Automatic program verification I: A logical basis and its implementation. *Acta Informatica,* 4 (2): 145-182.

Katz, S. M., and Z. Manna (Aug. 1973). A heuristic approach to program verification. In *Proceedings of the Third International Conference on Artificial Intelligence,* Stanford University, Stanford, Ca., pp. 143-155.

Katz, S. M., and Z. Manna (1975). A closer look at termination. *Acta Informatica*, 5 (4): 333–352.

Katz, S. M., and Z. Manna (Apr. 1976). Logical analysis of programs. *CACM*, 19 (4): 188–206. (The second paper in this collection.)

King, J. C. (1969). *A Program Verifier.* Ph.D. thesis. Carnegie-Mellon University, Pittsburgh, Pa.

King, J. C. (1970). A verifying compiler. In *Debugging Techniques in Large Systems* (Randall Rustin, ed.), Englewood Cliffs, N.J.: Prentice-Hall, pp. 17–39.

Knuth, D. E. (1968). *The Art of Computer Programming, Volume 1: Fundamental Algorithms.* Reading, Mass: Addison-Wesley.

Knuth, D. E. (1969). *The Art of Computer Programming, Volume 2: Seminumerical Algorithms.* Reading, Mass: Addison-Wesley.

Kowlaski, R. (March 1974). *Logic for Problem Solving.* Technical report. University of Edinburgh, Edinburgh.

Luckham, D. C., and N. Suzuki (Oct. 1975). *Proof of Termination within a Weak Logic of Programs,* Technical report. Stanford University, Stanford, Ca.

Manna, Z. (May 1969). The correctness of programs. *JCSS*, 3 (2): 119–127.

Manna, Z. (1974). *Mathematical Theory of Computation.* New York: McGraw-Hill.

Manna, Z., and A. Pnueli (July 1970). Formalization of properties of functional programs. *JACM*, 17 (3): 555–569.

Manna, Z., and R. Waldinger (March 1971). Toward automatic program synthesis. *CACM*, 14 (3): 151–165.

Manna, Z., and R. Waldinger (1975). Knowledge and reasoning in program synthesis. *Artificial Intelligence*, 6 (2): 175–208. (The third paper in this collection.)

McCarthy, J. (1962). Towards a mathematical science of computation. In *Information Processing, Proceedings of IFIP Congress 1962* (C. M. Popplewell, ed.). Amsterdam: North-Holland, pp. 21–28.

McCarthy, J., P. W. Abrahams, D. J. Edwards, T. P. Hart, and M. I. Levin (Aug. 1962). *LISP 1.5 Programmer's Manual.* Cambridge, Mass.: M.I.T. Press,

Naur, P. (1966). Proof of algorithms by general snapshots. *BIT*, 6: 310–316.

Robinson, J. A. (Jan. 1965). A machine oriented logic based on the resolution principle. *JACM*, 12 (1): 23–41.

Rulifson, J. F., J. A. Derksen, and R. J. Waldinger (Nov. 1972). *QA4: A Procedural Calculus for Intuitive Reasoning.* Technical report. Stanford Research Institute, Menlo Park, Ca.

Siklòssy, L. (Nov. 1974). The synthesis of programs from their properties, and the insane heuristic. In *Proceedings of the Third Texas Conference on Computing Systems,* Austin, Texas.

Simon, H. A. (Oct. 1963). Experiments with a heuristic compiler. *JACM,* 10 (4): 493–506.

Sites, R. L. (May 1974). *Proving that Computer Programs Terminate Cleanly.* Ph.D. thesis. Stanford University, Stanford, Ca.

Summers, P. D. (Jan. 1976). A methodology for LISP program construction from examples. In *Proceedings of the Third ACM Symposium on Principles of Programming Languages,* Atlanta, Ga., pp. 68–76.

Sussman, G. J. (1975). *A Computer Model of Skill Acquisition.* New York: Elsevier North-Holland.

Suzuki, N. (Apr. 1975). Verifying programs by algebraic and logical reduction. In *Proceedings of the International Conference on Reliable Software,* Los Angeles, Ca., pp. 473–481.

Teitelman, W. (Dec. 1975). *INTERLISP Reference Manual,* Xerox PARC, Palo Alto, Ca.

Turing, A. M. (Jan. 1950). Checking a large routine. In *Report of a Conference on High Speed Automatic Calculating Machines,* University of Toronto, Canada, pp. 66–69.

von Neumann, J., and H. H. Goldstine (1963). Planning and coding problems for an electronic computer instrument, Part 2. In *Collected Works of John von Neumann.* vol. 5, New York: Macmillan, pp. 91–99.

Waldinger, R. J. (1977). Achieving several goals simultaneously. In *Machine Intelligence 8: Machine Representations of Knowledge* (E. W. Elcock and D. Michie, eds.). New York: John Wiley and Sons, Inc.

Waldinger, R. J., and R. C. T. Lee (May 1969). PROW: A step toward automatic program writing, In *Proceedings of International Joint Conference on Artificial Intelligence,* Washington, D.C., pp. 241–252.

Waldinger, R. J., and K. N. Levitt (1974). Reasoning about programs. *Artificial Intelligence,* 5: 235–316.(The first paper in this collection.)

Warren, D. H. D. (June 1976). *Warplan: A System for Generating Plans.* Memo. University of Edinburgh, Edinburgh, Scotland.

Wegbreit, B. (Feb. 1974). The synthesis of loop predicates. *CACM*, 17 (2): 163–167.

Wegbreit, B. (Sept. 1975). Mechanical program analysis. *CACM*, 18 (9): 528–539.

Wensley, J. H. (1958). A class of non-analytical interactive processes. *Computer Journal*, 1: 163–167.

Wilber, B. M. (March 1976). A QLISP Reference Manual. Technical report. Stanford Research Institute, Menlo Park, Ca.

Name Index

Abrahams, P.W., 15,22

Balzer, R.M., 143
Biermann, A.W., 142,180
Bledsoe, W.W., 93,179
Boyer, R.S., 1,147
Buchanan, J.R., 177
Burstall, R.M., 148,177,

Cooper, D.C., 139

Darlington, J., 148,177,180
Derksen, J.A.C., 2,38,176
Deutsch, L.P., 1,30,93

Edwards, D.J., 15,22
Elspas, B., 2,7,139

Floyd, R.W., 3,8,37,93,121,124,139,
140,152

German, S.M., 7,179
Goldstine, H.H., 3
Good, D.I., 93,179
Green, C., 176,177
Greif, I., 139

Hardy, S., 142
Hart, T.P., 15,22
Hein, P., 1
Hewitt, C., 13,142,143
Hoare, C.A.R., 1,3,28,30,35,152

Igarashi, S., 1,30

Katz, S.M., 7,126,139
King, J.C., 1,19,35,36,93,139
Kowalski, R., 143
Knuth, D.E., 3,15,139
Krishnaswamy, R., 142

Lee, R.C.T., 176
Levin, M.I., 15 22
Levitt, K.N., 2,93,139
London, R.L., 1,30,93,179
Luckham, D.C., 1,30,177,179

Manna, Z., 7,25,96,119,126,139,146,
176
McCarthy, J., 15,19,22
Moore, J.S., 1,147

Naur, P., 3
von Neumann, J., 3

Pnueli, A., 25

Reboh, R., 36
Robinson, J.A., 22,23,157,171
Rulifson, J.F., 2,38,176

Sacerdoti, E.D., 36
Siklossy, L., 180
Simon, H.A., 176
Sites, R.L., 139
Summers, P.D., 142

Subject Index